1019

Paul,

Embrace change, act with courage and
Keep Learning.
Write a glorious chapter in Harlad's
rich history book.

Jaymes

"one lousy mouse"

Winners Are Not Lonely At The Top

A Live Case Study to Inspire Leaders Worldwide

Carl Phillips and Jacques Seguin

Copyright © 2012 by Carl Phillips and Jacques Seguin
First Edition – December 2012

ISBN
978-1-4602-0841-0 (Hardcover)
978-1-4602-0839-7 (Paperback)
978-1-4602-0840-3 (eBook)

All rights reserved.

No part of this publication may be reproduced in any form, or by any means, electronic or mechanical, including photocopying, recording, or any information browsing, storage, or retrieval system, without permission in writing from the publisher.

Produced by:

FriesenPress
Suite 300 – 852 Fort Street
Victoria, BC, Canada V8W 1H8

www.friesenpress.com

Distributed to the trade by The Ingram Book Company

Dedication

Jointly dedicated to....

Jacques – to my parents Andre and Clairette, my wife Michele and my children, Jacob and Jared.

~

Carl – to my wife Maureen, my daughter Alison and her husband Michael, my son Shane and my grandchildren Troy and Ashley.

Table of Contents

Table of Contents

Winners Are Not Lonely At The Top

"[The] Five Star Power process enabled us to turn around a global professional services firm whose revenues had stalled... without this platform for change, we simply would not have made it."

Paul Daoust, Former Chief Operating Officer,
Watson Wyatt Worldwide, Boston, USA.

~

"This has given our company a proven process for leading our people into the 21st Century."

John Donaldson, Managing Director,
The Thomas Cook Group, London, UK.

~

"The process helped Ultragaz establish and operationalize a global vision. This process helped us coalesce the executive team around the vision and aggressively champion the implementation through a comprehensive set of actions and measures."

Paulo Cunha, President and CEO,
Ultragaz, Sao Paulo, Brazil.

~

"The process helped us succeed. No question."

K. Linn Macdonald, President and CEO,
Noranda Forest Inc, Toronto, Canada.

Foreward

Paul Daoust, Former Chief Operating
Officer Watson Wyatt Worldwide

When my colleague, advisor and friend, Carl Phillips, asked me to write the Foreward for this book, I immediately agreed. I would do most anything for Carl after he saved my hide (and our firm's) with his change management protocols and processes in the 1990's. His Five Star Power process enabled us to turn around a global professional services firm whose revenues had stalled and profits had dropped in somewhat dramatic fashion, creating the classic "burning platform" for change. It is easy to look back now and understand that without this platform for change we simply would not have made it. What is harder to do is describe in a succinct way what actually happened.

A few paragraphs summarizing the challenges we faced in 1993 might be helpful. We were one of the world's largest human resource consulting firms, about $ 500 million in 1993 dollars, with about 3,500 associates in eighty offices located in thirty-five countries around the world. True to our heritage, we were organized in a decentralized fashion, with about half of our offices having been started through the acquisition of a local firm, resulting in a somewhat thin culture. Nevertheless, we were a proud firm with a high level of camaraderie where innovation, professionalism, and entrepreneurship were clearly valued and encouraged.

We had outstanding consulting talent across nine practice areas but there were no global (or even national) protocols on consulting techniques, data, or tools. The business was really run by the eighty Office Managers, or OM, (I had been the OM in both Boston and New York). The local office financials were the single most important metric in the firm, driving each office's piece of the company compensation and stock pie with little financial incentive to work across offices. The OM had the final say on who got what within their profit center, full stop. As an Office Manager you also had your own functions around IT, finance, HR, training, etc., and you decided what class of office space you had, how long your lease would be, and how much you would spend on the latest and greatest technology (which was into the millions of dollars in some cases). There were no non-competes in place so if an OM was terminated, he could take consultants and clients across the street, set up a competitive shop, and still get the full payout on company stock. It wasn't a franchise like many of our competitors liked to describe it, but it was close.

It was an excellent model for the first forty-five years of the business when entrepreneurship was critical, the IT spend was low, and clients were more locally oriented. In 1993 we were still producing outstanding, innovative, and creative consulting, but the model had become problematic as our clients became more global, requiring multinational teams delivering consulting with consistent protocols across the world. Meanwhile we were often reinventing the wheel over and over again on what was getting to be very expensive technology platforms. Finally the redundancy in our staffing infrastructure was obvious and we had most of our chips bet on the local OM who had to deliver across nine practice areas, mostly on her own, leading to inconsistent (at best) financial results across offices and thus, the firm.

When I became COO in 1993, it was time to turn the ship in the direction of the "one firm firm", but it wasn't one big aircraft carrier – – it was eighty PT boats. But all eighty OM's reported to me so this would be simple, right? Wrong. The OM's had almost complete control of their business, so I was in charge of everything but really had control of almost nothing. This is when I turned to Carl for his ideas on creating a platform for change.

Carl's Preface indicates that leaders fail at their jobs often by failing to engage their people because they either lack awareness (we didn't), lack a process (we sure did), or the process takes too much self-awareness and self-discipline (this was the big unknown at the outset). With Carl's guidance we set up a process which included all eighty leaders worldwide coming together and agreeing that we had a problem that had to be solved but could only be done with the creative involvement of all of them. We went at it in waves by major regions of the world, but always involving worldwide representation so the key leaders knew what was taking place across the company.

They effectively gave up considerable control to the center, as it were, to allow the reorganization of the company from top to bottom. We threw out the absolute bedrock of the local office financials and imposed a matrix structure of practice leaders responsible for global practice strategies and protocols and regional managers responsible for execution across all the offices in their respective regions. For the first time in history (other than through acquisition), we recruited heavily outside for management talent experienced in leading across geographies to the extent that half of our seventeen person senior management matrix was new to the company. Over fifty senior leaders had changes in their positions in the first three years, all by following a blueprint for change that they themselves effectively developed. This was leaders being leaders, all trying to do the right thing for the organization. This was Five Star Power in action.

The results were impressive. Despite all of the above referenced changes in leadership, over five years our global consulting operations doubled revenues and tripled profits (two record years at the end). We rebranded the company, accomplished a major blue chip partnership with Watson's in the UK, and provided for nine figures of investment for our human resource outsourcing business. There's no way you can get this done by memos from headquarters in a decentralized global business where the local leaders own the business. Without the platform of trust and mutual respect that Carl's process enabled, it would simply never have happened.

So read on and enjoy yourself, listening to Professor Carl telling you how to do it and Student Jacques, who, like me, tried the Professor's recommended experiments and liked the results. Be ready for a lot of learning and a relentless process, which is the way it has to be. Real change is extremely hard and it will take leadership from you and from many others to achieve meaningful results.

Once you go down the road of Five Star Power, whatever you do, don't blink.

Preface

Winners Are Not Lonely At The Top
With Five Star Power

Are you lonely at the top? Do you want to replace that loneliness with the thrill of experiencing exponential growth in your organization that is driven by an excited and totally committed well-oiled team? If so, read on. Several leaders have successfully done it using Five Star Power, the theme of this book. All we can say to help you read further and absorb the process for your own development is that the process is time honoured and proven to work again and again.

Is another book on leadership required when the bookstores are overflowing with books on the topic? Yes, because most leaders still don't get it or do not apply it. "Don't get what?" you ask. They don't get the fact that their pre-eminent role is to concentrate on creating more leaders rather than followers in their organizations.

Most leaders would say, "I knew that," to this answer. Why then do I say that they don't get it? True leaders know that their first and foremost role is to empower and inspire their employees so that the employees are totally involved and committed to the goals of the organization. They get them totally engaged in the organization. Yet extensive research in the USA reveals that more than 50% of employees are **not** engaged at work and, in fact, as many as 20% are actively disengaged, resulting in several hundred billion dollars in lost productivity.

On the other hand, engaged people in an organization mentally consider themselves owners of the business and function as such. They become totally involved and, being mutually responsible and accountable, they passionately drive the organization to a commonly shared vision. This book tells of several organizations that have applied the Five Star Power process and achieved such a state of engagement of its employees.

Why then do leaders stop short of truly engaging their employees? Does this mean that leaders in general do not comprehend the meaning of people "being engaged" in their work, or does it mean that leaders find it too cumbersome and complex to deal with? In my thirty-five years of consulting as an Organization Effectiveness Consultant to Senior Executives in North America, Europe and Asia, I would have to say that most leaders underestimate the overwhelming power and force of a group of people being totally engaged and committed to making things happen in the workplace. It doesn't take too much imagination for a leader to visualize the force generated by several leaders like themselves functioning in tandem with the same passion and commitment. If they as leaders can make a major difference in an organization, how much more of an impact would several leaders of the same ilk do? More importantly, leaders who intrinsically understand the importance of people being engaged in their work are hungry for any system or process that will help them engage their people. Therefore we have any number of processes or systems that are constantly on the market, but few that address this blind spot of leadership.

Do leaders fail to concentrate on getting their people totally engaged in their work because of a lack of a process? Or is it because of a lack of awareness? Or is it because it takes too much self-awareness and self-discipline? Interestingly enough, it is because of all three above.

This Book defines a comprehensive approach that encompasses these three ingredients working in tandem and the implementation of which has greatly increased employee involvement in several live organizations with excellent performance results. The process is enunciated in five simple steps referred to as **FIVE STAR POWER.**

In this book we have the President of one such company, Jacques Seguin, who implemented the process. He describes what he did and tells us how he and his leaders helped create a success story in the much beleaguered manufacturing sector in North America. I was the consultant who worked closely with his team as they made this happen.

Jacques Seguin's business philosophy is completely in sync with the philosophy of the Five Star Power process. Jacques has over twenty five years of experience in leading organizations through Change, Revitalization, and Profitable Global Growth.

As President of the Garland Group, a more than $150 million organization with a distribution network of a hundred countries worldwide, Jacques led a team that achieved sales improvement of 52% over four years and consistent organic growth of 11.5%, which accelerated to 19% in 2008. His team outperformed their industry growth rate by more than three times.

Some statistics might help picture this growth more clearly:

- Improvements of 545% in EBITA and 460% in cash over

seven years.

- During this time the company invested $10 million in capital expenditures and new product development.

- This investment resulted in three industry leading innovation awards in twelve months.

- His team was the first ever in their field to win the Canadian Food Service and Hospitality Pinnacle Award.

Jacques achieved these results while implementing the processes outlined in this book.

As President of an organization effectiveness consulting company, I concentrated on the development of processes that would help leaders engage their people in their work environments by clarifying and dealing head on with reality. The success of my company in North America prompted me to sell my organization to a global company, Watson Wyatt Worldwide. I became the head of the Global Organization Effectiveness Practice for Watson Wyatt Worldwide. In this capacity I consulted with CEOs and leaders all around the world. In fact, I co-authored a book for which we interviewed seventy-five CEOs of global companies from twenty-eight countries, titled *Global Literacies*.

One of my main assignments as head of the Organization Effectiveness Practice for Watson Wyatt Worldwide was to work closely with the Chief Executive Officer and the Chief Operating Officer to apply this process to Watson Wyatt Worldwide itself. Watson Wyatt at the time (1993) was a privately owned international company with three main regions: the Americas, Europe, and Asia Pacific, with a total workforce of 3500 employees.

The process was applied in stages; first to the Americas, then Europe, and lastly Asia Pacific. Embedding this process in the company took approximately five years. The main driver for the process was the Chief Operating Officer, who believed in the concept and worked with the senior executive team zealously. He and the senior executive team worked tirelessly to embed the process in the organization. This is a key prerequisite because the process is basically a leader driven approach.

The company's performance during that period increased so dramatically, both in top and bottom line, that the company had little difficulty in going public very soon after this. Even more impressive is the fact that the process and related practices took such strong root in the company that while being supported with continued strong leadership, the organization expanded exponentially and finally merged with its chief competitor, Towers Perrin, to form Towers Watson in 2010-a 3.2 billion dollar corporation, now one of the largest management consulting firms in the world with over 14,000 employees in thirty-five countries. This is a true success story of leaders genuinely engaging people to create a great company.

I have personally assisted in the implementation of many such projects over the years with similar results. The thrill and satisfaction that one gets when an organization starts firing on all cylinders prompted both Jacques and I to write this do-it-yourself book for leaders everywhere. We wanted them to experience the pleasure of flying with the eagles as their organizations soar among the world's top performers.

The Five Star Power process shows leaders how to process and integrate the leader's thinking and expectations with every single person of the organization so that there is a concerted, clearly directed force driving the execution of the business strategy. While the process might at times seem challenging and demanding because people need time to process ideas and enthusiastically get on the bus, it is extremely rewarding and satisfying for everyone involved when effectively implemented. In fact, once the new corporate culture begins to take root, it is the start of the evolution of a great organization as described by Jim Collins in his book *Good to Great*.

Carl Phillips

Jacques Seguin

Chapter One

Introduction
Five Star Power
For Life's Unwritten Rules of Engagement

Life looks just a little more mathematical and regular than it is. Its exactitude is obvious, but its inexactitude is hidden; its wildness lies in wait."

G. K. Chesteron

There has never been a greater need for true leaders. The current financial crisis has left people disillusioned and distrustful of leaders at all levels. Whose words can one trust if the most conservative leaders of banks and government regulatory bodies have dropped the ball, leaving us on the brink of disaster? What will re-establish trust and confidence in leaders? This question should be at the front of every leader's mind as they wrestle with this lack of confidence and trust in their leadership.

This book is written based on certain assumptions about life's unwritten rules of engagement that need to be clarified and stated even though some of it deals with repeating the obvious. For example, while it is obvious that people make things happen in life, this fact is seldom employed effectively as a tool by leaders to raise the performance of their organizations.

Have you asked yourself what makes an organization a global leader? In our book *Global Literacies* we interviewed seventy-eight CEOs of leading global companies with 3.5 million employees in two hundred countries to identify what made them succeed in a global setting. The key answer: people. What makes people do things above and beyond the call of duty? Leaders.

By and large, CEOs are extremely dedicated people with very good intentions who are able to excite people toward a vision. Unfortunately for them and the people they lead, a majority of CEOs have one big blind spot: they seriously believe that it is up to them alone to develop a vision for the organization and also to implement that vision alone! Thus they confirm in their minds that it is lonely at the top. It does not have to be so with Five Star Power.

They toil eighteen to nineteen hours a day, seven days a week, with almost maniacal zeal to dot every "I" and cross every "T" to ensure that the organization prospers. They even toss and turn through the night, looking for solutions to some problem that one of their leaders is currently facing. They try to be involved in either doing things themselves or helping a direct report to do it. They feel guilty if they take a day off because they are under the weather. They genuinely believe their people really need their support as they micromanage them as much as their official twelve-hour day will permit. Some even pride themselves on not taking any vacations. Naturally then, they tend to feel that they are giving of their best and often are oblivious of the fact that their people, meanwhile, are frustrated and stifled because they feel that they are not being given the opportunity to be innovative and creative. We know because we've been there.

People make things happen in an organization, not products, services, or markets. People drive all of the above. This sounds like a blinding flash of the obvious. I know most leaders will say that this is not news to them; they understand that people can make or break the organization. If this is true, then why do we have such a small number of people–less than 50%-- that are truly engaged in their work in the USA, a country that leads the industrialized world in business performance? I think that leaders need to take another look at their true purpose in leading an organization.

Leaders first and foremost need to be trusted and respected as someone whose word is their bond. How does a leader do this? The leader generates trust and confidence when the leader walks the talk. The leader does what she says she will do and is completely transparent in how she does it. This is an unavoidable first step for the leader.

Thereafter the leader's job is to articulate the common vision of the organization (a vision that is enthusiastically shared by every person in the organization) and then energize, inspire, and empower the people to zealously and persistently seek to achieve that vision. To do this the leader needs the help of other leaders who are as committed and passionate about achieving the vision. Knowing these facts and putting them into practice calls upon a very different skill-set in a leader: the courage of their convictions to deal effectively with reality and a true understanding of people dynamics.When I was called in to consult in an organization, I was often faced with the fact that the leader already knew what the problem was in the organization and also, in some cases, what needed to be done to solve the problem. Most often they hesitated because of two reasons: their hesitance to deal with reality and the subsequent unknown fallout in people dynamics.

It's common knowledge that the majority of business plans fail because of poor execution, and poor execution is mainly a function of poor leadership and ineffective utilization of people. So what do most CEOs do? Out of the goodness of their hearts and the belief that they can do it better than anyone else in the organization, (which is probably true, and if so then they have a serious shortage of talent) they try to do everything themselves. Even worse, they micromanage every step of the execution of the business plan – – a guaranteed formula for making one awfully lonely at the top.

This book tells you in simple words and processes how to effectively deal with these intangible, though very real, dynamics. Leaders, who have inculcated the lessons enumerated in this book into their organizations, have achieved unprecedented results. What is even better is that they have personally developed into better leaders, capable of inspiring their teams onto extraordinary performances that are self-sustaining. They create even better leaders.

One of the key functions of a leader is to help people understand, accept, and deal with reality in the workplace. How can they do this when they themselves don't know how to deal with reality? Through our book you will learn how to personally face reality as you implement the first of the Five Star Power processes. There are three distinct steps in facing reality:

- Objectively analyse the facts of the situation and clearly understand them.

- Accept the facts as the reality of the situation.

- Have the courage of your convictions to effectively deal with the situation.

Secondly, you as a leader have to deal with people dynamics. What do we mean by people dynamics? All that is involved when a leader influences and is being influenced by all the people in the organization. This is different from allotting a person a task and making sure the person does it. It deals with feelings, emotions, and the commitment of people individually and as a group. It is the difference that motivates a person who wins a race with the same physical capabilities as the person who loses the race by mere inches. It's the winner's edge. It's in the winner's mind that the race is won. This book tells you how to deal with people dynamics.

In order to make things happen in the organization through people, they must understand the consequence of every action that they take and the impact it has on every person working within that particular team and the overall impact on the achievement of the vision.

When we deal with leadership or management, what does the phrase, "its wildness lies in wait," mean in the quotation from G.K. Chesterton above? We are dealing with a very complex mechanism known as the human mind. Take the human mind for granted using pure logic and the meaning of life's "wildness lying in wait" will become immediately apparent. Work with the human mind's complexity and seek to understand its softer idiosyncratic perspective on intellectual, emotional, cultural, motivational, and self-fulfillment needs, and you begin to understand how to harness unfathomable depths of human energy – – energy that will inspire extraordinary achievements from otherwise ordinary people.

When you face people with the brutal facts that represent reality, they have some common responses, which should not deter you in your efforts to help them recognize the harbingers of the evolving reality. Responses such as:

- This will have no impact on us because we are different.

- We have been here before and survived.

- This is a minor blip that will go away.

- You are pushing the panic button unnecessarily.

- If we ignore it, maybe somebody else will take care of it.

- I do not want to be the one who delivers the brutal facts.

- I know what I must do, but I am not sure that I can live with the fallout from my actions.

Also, to be the "Reality Person" you must be able to articulate the change in understandable terms and help evolve a viable course of action. Most leaders have difficulty in articulating the evolving reality in such a manner that their audience can interpret what they say in the identical form as visualized by the leader. With every statement that introduces change, the leader envisages a goodly amount of emotional commitment, social and behavioural adjustment, and in some cases the relinquishing of privileges and entitlements as the success of the organization becomes the top priority.

One only has to see the enormous resistance that leaders in Europe are facing as they seek to have the people accept the reality of the present day financial crisis to truly comprehend how people are often surprised and annoyed by the accompanying adjustments to the new rules of engagement. They do not interpret the change in the same way that the leader has. More importantly, if the leader's interpretation is based on reality and universal truisms, and the people in the organization are not on the same frequency, the situation becomes even more cumbersome for the leader and subsequently stifles the performance of the organization. The leaders need to help the people connect the dots.

Often the leaders do not have a good grasp of the situation and therefore they are incapable of connecting the dots in a clear and simplistic manner. If you have ever tried to teach someone else a complex concept, you will know that you have to truly understand the complex concept yourself before you can teach it in an understandable form. In fact, if the leader is capable of describing the situation simplistically and clearly, several benefits accrue from this action.

- The leader becomes more aware of the true issues and the realistic possible solutions.

- The people being addressed are immediately onside and are not second guessing the leader's intentions.

- The clarity and simplicity in the communication makes it much easier and faster for creating and implementing a corrective action plan.

- The people are gradually sensitized to the complexity and insidiousness of the evolving reality.

Then again there are those who are attuned to the changing circumstances and are quite aware of the deteriorating situation, but they are unable to react. They suffer from paralysis by analysis. They need someone or some situations to kick-start them. They need a process and an enlightened leader that will help them simplify the situation and clarify the evolving reality. Once this happens, the impasse is broken and moving forward is easier.

There are five distinct steps, each representing a STAR (hence the name Five Star Power) that every successful leader must follow in order to manage reality and the dynamics in the organization's people:

- When a business leader is faced with rapid change, the leader should personally accept the change no matter how ugly and undesirable it may seem to set an example for the rest of the organization, especially where the change requires a major change in the leader's operating style. The leader must walk the talk. This is probably the toughest challenge any leader will ever face. Most leaders know this, and often this is the reason why they hesitate to acknowledge and clearly articulate the need for change. The leader must Start by facing reality - the first star of the five star process.

- The leader must be able to clearly and succinctly articulate the common vision of the organization to encompass the changing business landscape. The leader must be able to communicate this message to every member of the organization in such a manner that they are able to connect the dots back to the impact on their individual contributions. This should help people to personally understand and accept the change, and thus inspire them to be committed to deal with it. The leader must **T**arget the common vision - the second star of the five star process.

- The leader must embed team values in the organization that encourage every team member to internalize the concept of mutual accountability and responsibility. The leader must **A**ssemble mutually supportive teams - the third star of the five star process.

- The leader must be able to entrench a disciplined culture of results oriented team work that is consistently and persistently applied to any necessary corrective action that will help restore the competitive status of the organization. The leader must **R**eward a disciplined culture -the fourth star of the five star process.

- The leader should believe in the philosophy that the true purpose of a leader is to create more leaders. This belief drives the leader to cascade innovative leadership thinking down to the lowest level of the organization. This then becomes the bedrock on which the organization continues to sustain a superior leadership position in the world. The leader must **S**eek and **S**eed leaders for all levels of the organization - the fifth and last star of the five star process.

The above critical steps are the central theme of this book – FIVE STAR POWER. In order to implement these themes, it is necessary to embed each theme in an organization through a step by step sequential proven process. We believe that every time a leader achieves each step of the process, the leader has achieved a star.

Each of these themes will be described in detail so that every leader who reads this book will be in a position to personally implement the process. All that a leader will require is the self-discipline to meticulously follow the processes, whether they apply to the leader or to the rest of the organization, persistently and consistently. Most operational change regimens fail because of the lack of constancy in the follow-through.

This book describes the process as it was successfully applied to the Garland Group of Companies. While the experience with Garland is specific to a manufacturing environment, the process has been successfully applied to large service companies, distribution organizations, technology companies, government organizations, and retail businesses.

This is a proven process that has been applied successfully to many companies internationally both large and small over three decades with unprecedented positive results. The book documents a specific company's experience in the application of this process and the resultant benefits to every single leader in the organization. It takes one through the experience with the resultant pitfalls and lessons learned that serves as a guide for any CEO interested in creating a great organization. More importantly, it is a step-by-step process for a business to deal effectively with the white knuckle pace of the present day evolution of reality and through it all be able to sustain a superior leadership role in its chosen field.

The book documents the challenges faced by Jacques Seguin and his team as he applies the process over a four year period. It provides a real-life snapshot of the typical issues that leaders face in all organizations, irrespective of size, type, or purpose of the organization. The two common factors here are people and leaders. The book is an amalgam of theory, process, and effective application of leadership in action as it systematically deals with the whole spectrum of leading organizational change in a mushrooming global setting. The following chapters will show an outline of the theory and processes recommended to deal with each of the five bulleted requirements or stars for leaders to follow in order to run a great company and Jacques will describe the resultant outcomes when he implemented these processes in the Garland Group.

Summary of the Introduction

This book has been written with certain basic assumptions:

- Today the re-establishment of trust in leadership is badly needed.

- People are taken for granted and often valued less than markets, products, systems, and processes.

- True critical underpinnings of global success are people and leaders.

- Leadership's blind spot: leaders feel that they have to do everything in an organization and are often lonely at the top.

- People make things happen in organizations-not markets, products, and services.

- Leaders need to deal effectively with reality and people dynamics.

- People normally avoid or ignore reality and life's unwritten rules of engagement.

- People need some process to kick start them to deal with these issues.

- The Five Star process helps a leader to do just this. There are five distinct steps represented by the acronym STARS.

- Start facing reality.

- Target a common vision.

- Assemble a mutually supporting team.

- Reward a disciplined culture.

- Seek and seed leaders at all levels of an organization.

The book details a live case study of the application of the Five Star process to the Garland Group by Jacques Seguin and Carl Phillips and how they achieved unprecedented results.

Key Message

Leadership's key function is to create more leaders who in turn will drive markets, products, systems, services, and profits. Leaders and the led are jointly responsible and accountable.

Chapter Two

The Need

"I could live for two months on a good compliment."

Mark Twain

In the previous chapter, based on extensive research, we have stated emphatically that the two main players responsible for helping an organization achieve greatness are leaders and the people they lead. Exceptional leader's help people achieve exceptional results and thus create great organizations. Making exceptional things happen through people requires us to understand what makes ordinary people do extraordinary things. Exceptional leaders understand this intrinsically. Those who do not grasp the mechanics and dynamics involved are often left struggling with a mediocre performance in the work place. Often the reason that these issues are ignored is that they seem to be trivial or just window dressing and therefore not that important. Let me explain this through a real life example of the mechanics and dynamics at play in an organization.

A CEO walks into an elevator at the start of a work day with a lot on his mind concerning a problem that had nothing to do with a Vice President of the company, who was also in the elevator. Because the CEO was preoccupied with this problem, the Vice President was inadvertently ignored and the CEO did not even acknowledge the VP's friendly "Hi". The CEO got off at his floor and walked away into his office, totally oblivious of the dynamics that he had generated.

The VP, on the other hand, was devastated because she had wrongly interpreted the CEO's behaviour as a form of disapproval of her for some work related issue that she had fouled up. Worse still, could it be something personal over which he was annoyed? Normally the CEO was very cordial and friendly with her whenever they met.

The VP went about her job that day with half of her mind being preoccupied with the elevator incident. She spent the next two hours reviewing in great detail all projects with her subordinates with this incident in mind. The VP then cautiously checked with the other VPs to see if they were aware if something had upset the CEO and found nothing of significance. She accordingly wasted the better part of the morning on tenterhooks and worry as she reviewed all her interactions with the CEO over the last few days to see if she had inadvertently slighted him personally. She was very sensitive and aware of her impact on people and could not rest till she could explain the cause of the CEO's behaviour. You can therefore imagine how productive she was that morning and what it cost the organization as she was considered one of the top executives of the company and was always greeted warmly by the CEO and other senior executive members.

Just before lunch that morning, the CEO walked into the VP's office and congratulated her on doing an excellent job on a recent project and went on to say that the company was fortunate to have such a conscientious and dedicated employee. The VP was surprised by the compliment and could not resist asking the CEO why he was so aloof towards her in the elevator that morning. The CEO did not seem to know what she was talking about. In fact, he was very apologetic about his apparent behaviour and explained that he may have behaved like that because he was preoccupied with a very valued client's problems.

This incident might look like the description of an individual overreacting to the CEO's behaviour, though unfortunately it's these subtle aspects of the behaviour of leaders that ignite or subdue the behaviour of people in an organization. What does this incident tell us? Several important messages that constitute people dynamics are at play around the mechanics of running a business. The CEO was transmitting negative vibes by his behaviour that caused a very productive employee to waste the better part of a morning in unproductive activities and low morale. We can draw the following lessons about people dynamics in an organization from this incident.

- The leader's behaviour is more powerful than any words or messages that are communicated to the organization by the leader.

- The interpretation of the leader's behaviour is individually different for different people, and the behaviour is always being critically watched and analyzed and acted upon by the people of the organization.

- The dynamics triggered by a miscommunication can often cost the organization undue grief and consequent immeasurable losses in productivity.

- Leaders need to be sensitive to the feelings of the people in the organization at all times, whether they are addressing a specific organizational issue or dealing with a personal problem.

- A leader's good intentions mean nothing if the behaviour of the leader is transmitting a negative or dubious message.

- In essence, leaders need to have a realistic understanding of their own behaviour and be prepared to modify it, because the leader's behaviour serves as a model for the rest of the organization.

- Lastly, being oblivious of the impact of your behaviour on others as a leader is not an option, no matter how preoccupied one may be.

- The above gives one an idea of the impact that a leader's actions have on people. What does this mean for the leader? How can we use this knowledge to improve the performance of a leader and subsequently the performance of an organization?

A leader, by definition, leads. If one is to lead then one must initiate and promote positive action by:

- Recognizing and accepting the above impact that the leader's action has on people.

- Proactively modifying the negative behaviour to model the required positive behaviour.

- Creating trust in people through adhering consistently to

reality and the truisms of life.

- Inspiring the people onto bigger and greater achievements.

- Communicating honestly and effectively to the people of the organization.

- Walking the talk.

If a leader's job in an organization could be defined by three statements in the following manner.

The achievement of fixed goals	(Mechanics)
While adhering to defined procedures and processes and	(Mechanics)
While influencing and being influenced by the people, the business and the stakeholders of the organization	(Dynamics)

then the third statement (dynamics) above sums up where the bulk of the leader's attention needs to focus. Because the effectiveness with which the leader deals with the third statement, will determine how successfully statements 1 and 2 are achieved. What does this mean?

It means the leader's capability and willingness to influence and be influenced by the organization's environment is the key to the effective performance of an organization. Most ineffective leaders spend the majority of their efforts on micro-managing the mechanics (1 and 2 above), and ignoring statement 3. This leaves a trail of fear, stress, and low morale in their wake. While the leader is concentrating on the mechanics of performing the tasks based on the monitoring and enforcing of a pre-determined set of business rules, the people who have to implement these actions have to deal with several different dynamics at play around them as they deal with other people. The real life example of the interaction between the CEO and VP cited above is one such dynamic. If the leader is oblivious of the people dynamics inherent in the implementation of every mechanical process, then a feeling of distrust, fear, and uncertainty about the leadership will slowly poison the spirit of the organization, resulting in poor overall performance.

The mechanics of leadership are critical to the implementation of a plan of action. The mechanics mostly involves the applying of rules and processes and being able to deal with the nuances of business, such as business planning, product development, and operations planning. This is often manageable if it applies to one person doing a particular task. As one is given more and more responsibility for gaining results through people, things begin to become much more complicated and blurry. Just concentrating on the mechanics no longer works because now one has to deal with how other people see things and react to the achievement of the mechanics and dynamics. The results that one gains through the achievement of the mechanics are at the mercy of other people and their associated people dynamics. This is a more intangible, complex aspect of leadership that requires very sensitive and mature skills in a leader. It draws on a leader's ability to pragmatically discern the impact of several variables at once, such as:

- The motivational aspects of the action that is required.

- The fairness of the request for action.

- The capability of the team to carry out the action.

- The alignment of the action with the stated vision and values of the organization.

These are only a few of the possible permutations and combinations of the variables that can disrupt the momentum of the organization through the dynamics of the lack of trust, confidence, and team effort in the leadership. If a leader's behaviour ignores the impact of these variables, then the leader is clearly out of touch with the truisms of life and reality. Fig 1 shows clearly the difference between a leader's use of mechanics and dynamics.

MECHANICS	DYNAMICS
Operating Forces	Driving Forces
Logical	Implicit/Unstated
What and How	Why
Clear Agenda	Unstated Agenda
Infrastructure	Superstructure
More Tangible	More Intangible
Practical and Easier	Abstract and Very Difficult

So the most important need of an organization for it to stand out as great lies in the organization ensuring that the leaders, in addition to being proficient in the mechanics of leadership, are capable and effective in dealing with the reality of people dynamics. The extent to which leaders in the organization are people dynamics conscious will often determine the level of the organization. To put it in the form of a truism, an organization's performance cannot rise above the current level of the leadership of the organization. In other words, if you want to create a great company then the most important ingredient that you need to have is great leadership. That sounds like an obvious statement, but this truism is not always recognized and implemented in real life. The reason for this blind spot is that people dynamics are seldom truly understood, and if they are recognized, they seem to be too time consuming and complicated to apply. Most leaders who run into problems in this field take the short cut and drive roughshod on the mechanics. Often people will rightfully then accuse the leader of micro-managing.

Therefore, the first need that should be addressed in an organization that aspires to greatness is the behaviour of the leaders as it pertains to people dynamics, assuming that the mechanics are in place. If we consciously and consistently value this type of leadership, we will set the foundation for the creation of great leaders and thereby set the stage for the development of a great company.

What then do we mean by leaders who are "people dynamics" conscious? The simple answer is those leaders who understand what ordinary people need to achieve extraordinary results. Most ineffective leaders would claim that they have state of the art people management processes in place in their organizations, administered effectively by the human resources department. They then happily concentrate on the mechanics of the job, almost oblivious or avoiding the dynamics, with the hope that the human resources department is looking after the dynamics issues.

Most human resources people keep pulling their hair out because they are expected to deal with the underlying dynamics on their own, when the cause of the negative underlying dynamics is the senior executive who often mistakenly believes that people dynamics is the domain of the HR department. It takes a very brave human resource person to face the senior executive with the facts, if at all. Even then most leaders underestimate the power relating to people dynamics.

People are not impressed by words and processes; they want to know that their leaders are sensitive to their needs and have their feet firmly planted in reality and life's truisms. They are dealing with the brutal aspects of reality and life's truisms on a day to day basis and they need their leaders to roll up their sleeves and get into the trenches with them when the bullets are flying, not to be oblivious of their true issues and palm them off to the human resources department.

In my thirty-five years of consulting and managing a global consultancy, I have encountered a handful of CEOs and senior leaders who get these concepts on their own and are prepared to modify their behaviour to effectively deal with them. They see things naturally and do the right things spontaneously when dealing with people. In fact, some of them do the right things subconsciously, and they often find it difficult to explain their actions other than that they feel it is the right thing to do under the circumstances.

In such cases, more often than not, I have noticed that the spontaneous leader has internalized the mechanics and dynamics that make people tick by having learned most of these lessons the hard way, through personal experience. Of course there is the age old debate on the extent to which nature and nurture play a part in the final product, but we are really not concerned with the cause. Rather we are happy if the overall effect results in a leader tapping into the hidden resources of a virtual gold mine of people power. These leaders are a pleasure to work with.

Jacques Seguin is one such leader. Jacques has repeatedly shown that he has the raw gut feel required to deal with the reality and truisms of life. He has the integrity, fortitude, and courage of his convictions to do the right thing for the organization, despite the consequences to him or anyone else.

Over the last four years I have been coaching Jacques as he has led his organization through the management of people dynamics and he has seen the resultant rewards in both people performance and bottom-line output.

Why have I singled out Jacques Seguin's organization as an example of the effectiveness of the application of people dynamics when I have applied the same processes and techniques to much larger global companies with great success? The answer lies in the fact that the processes and techniques are equally effective in any organization, irrespective of the size or type of organization. This is because the processes and techniques deal with the two common ingredients of any organization: people and leaders.

More importantly, the size of the organization at the Garland Group lends itself to the ease of explaining and understanding these concepts that are often difficult to illustrate and track in a more complex organization. Also, Jacques has an intrinsic understanding of people dynamics and therefore provides a good base to draw on the experiences that have provided him with the needed insights and maturity to naturally encourage others to inculcate the same values and behaviours. By following his metamorphoses through his life experiences, maybe we can trigger dormant insights and behaviours in other leaders and thereby generate awareness in them that will help them blossom faster.

How did Jacques Seguin get it? He will tell you the full story in the next chapter.

Summary of the Chapter

- Exceptional leaders help ordinary people do extraordinary things, and thus create exceptional organizations.

- Exceptional leaders understand the mechanics and dynamics involved intrinsically, and therefore deal with each issue accordingly.

- The leader's behaviour is more powerful than any impassioned speeches or messages the leader makes.

- People are constantly watching the leader's behaviour and are sensitive to the slightest negative transmissions.

- The good intentions of a leader means nothing if the leader's behaviour is transmitting a negative or dubious message.

- The leader's behaviour serves as a model for the rest of the organization.

- Being oblivious of the impact of a leader's behaviour is not an option for a leader.

- Achieving goals while adhering to Life's truisms and facing reality is a basic foundation for good leadership.

- Leadership in business is defined as **achieving fixed goals while adhering to agreed upon processes and procedures(mechanics)** by **influencing and being influenced by the people, the business environment and the stakeholders (dynamics).**

Key Message

The level of a great company lies in the extent to which the leaders practice people dynamics while implementing the mechanics in the organization.

Chapter Three

The Roots of Jacques' Philosophy

Writing a book is one of the most difficult challenges that I have faced to date and at the same time it is also extremely rewarding. It starts a process of self-discovery and self-improvement. We all know that if you want to teach something, you have to first understand the subject matter before you try to teach it. In the process of understanding why you do what you do, you grow as an individual. As people and as leaders, we all have life experiences which have shaped our values, our beliefs, and subsequently, our behaviours. Boiling all of these experiences down to "my story" was a difficult task. When Carl and I met to define my role and deliverables for the book, he said, "Jacques, just tell your story. Find your teachable point of view and share it with other leaders who are struggling with the same issues that you face."

Carl's statement resonated with me based on my experiences with other leaders. I know of several leaders who are sincerely interested in making things happen in their organizations but are frustrated and often exhausted by the fact that they are working themselves to the bone and yet not getting what they know they should get. I know the feeling, because I've been there. I have lain awake many a night trying to define what I was missing or doing wrong as a leader that left me and my team feeling dissatisfied with our performances.

Interestingly enough, I eventually discovered that what I was missing did not require the use of rocket science. I needed to apply my foundational beliefs and values to my day-to-day living in order to help me and those I led to self-actualize and raise the bar of our performances. The question that evaded me was, how do I transfer what turned me on and made me totally committed to achieving my goals to all the people in the organization? It was clear that we needed a proven process to make this happen. That process is the core message of this book.

If through writing this book I can help my colleagues to experience the satisfaction of firing on all cylinders as a leader, which I feel I am beginning to do, then I will have made a difference. This approach can be adopted by any leader, no matter what type of organization, because it deals with two common factors that exist in every organization – -people and leaders.

Like most of us leaders, we have initially been very effective individual performers. We have been rewarded for our good performances by being made leaders with increasing responsibility until we wake up one day (if we're lucky) and find ourselves with the title of president of our organizations. When this happened to me, I could not have been happier and at the same time somewhat apprehensive because suddenly I was the boss and the buck stopped at my desk.

In keeping with my previous experience, my thoughts were, "I need to make a list of all the things that I need to do to get this organization moving. It is up to me to make things happen." This was not so bad when I was working with a portion of the company, but now I had the whole caboodle! With these thoughts came the realization that I was now very vulnerable because in the past I knew I could depend on myself in a crunch, but now I had to depend almost totally on other people to make things happen. So what did I do? I tried to do all the key jobs of the organization by micromanaging and constantly checking and rechecking the status of things. I had a finger on the pulse of all the issues and dictated most of the critical decisions. I was your traditional genius with a thousand helpers. Can you relate to this? If you can, then you must know how exhausted and frustrated you feel trying to make things happen. The difficult part about this situation was that, despite my frustration, the company was doing quite well and, therefore, it was lulling me into thinking that I was doing the right thing.

But somehow I knew in my heart that we were not on the right track. Eventually the cracks in the organization began to confirm my doubts.

- The slightest crisis required my input before a decision was made.

- I was spending most of my time on operations and very little time on strategy, my forte.

- I was working seven days a week and still felt that I was behind.

- People were working hard but basically doing what they were told to do.

- The employee satisfaction survey was not good. The majority of people did not have confidence in the management team, or in their direct supervisors.

- The management team was not really a team. They were polite and friendly with each other but they worked in their own silos.

- We all knew that we were not geared up sufficiently to deal with the global competition that was fast becoming a reality.

- Most importantly, we all were working at what we thought was our maximum capacity and therefore did not know how we could further cope with the faster and broader demands that we could see looming on the immediate horizon.

It was at this point that I sought help from Carl Phillips. Carl had a process through which he had helped several companies both large and small to raise their performance bar several levels higher to deal effectively with globalization. Carl and I had several conversations and it seemed to me that he was zeroing in on me as the first main issue to be addressed. Needless to say, this was somewhat threatening and demanding. While I knew that I would be required to adjust my behaviour, I didn't realize that I was the starting point. Nevertheless, what Carl was saying made good sense and I followed his instructions meticulously, however painful they seemed at first. I must admit that the process opened my eyes to my true responsibilities as the president of the organization. Once I adopted the new behaviour through the process, it was amazing how rewarding it was for me personally. Despite the initial resistance from the management team, they began to reap the multiple benefits of being a real team.

One of the first things that Carl challenged me to define was my life's experiences and my values in order for me to identify my behaviours. I thought long and hard to try to identify the things that had shaped my behaviours. In the end I came up with five things that stand out for me as foundational beliefs:

- Face your reality sooner rather than later. You will not avoid it by putting it off.

- Self-fulfillment comes from knowing how your values and beliefs were created and re-enforcing them no matter what.

- Families are stronger than teams. Treat your team as family.

- Courage propels desire into success. Extraordinary people are courageous people with extraordinary goals.

- Focus on winning. It's contagious.

There were other values that I learned as I grew up, but these stand out and have stood me in good stead throughout the years. How did I get them? I only have to look back to my formative years with my family and things become very clear. By me enumerating these circumstances, you, the reader, might be encouraged to do the same and thus be able to define your own teachable point of view. Someday you can share your story with others as I am now sharing mine. As you will see, my humble beginnings proved to be a strength rather than a weakness.

I was born and raised in a small Canadian town of Mattawa, which bordered on the provinces of Quebec and Ontario. With five brothers and three sisters, Mom and Dad faced difficult challenges every day. Providing for us all on a single income and keeping the peace among the siblings was a tough job. Dad worked two jobs while mom handled all the work associated with keeping the family going. She was battling cancer at the same time. Nevertheless, they shaped my thinking in very simple but effective ways by living these values on a day-to-day basis. The following excerpts from my earlier years will high-light the roots of my values and beliefs.

Face your reality sooner rather than later. You will not avoid it by putting it off.

Dad's use of "straight talk" and making us "face reality" was effective in managing our way through the challenging situations on a daily basis. He did not have time or the money to read books or hire consultants to help manage change. When Dad came home from work, Mom usually informed him of some problem that had come up that day. The septic system had overflowed, the washing machine was making a funny noise, or my brother had slammed his motorcycle into a fence. Whatever came his way, he would not spend a lot of time agonizing or feeling sorry for himself. He just got on with it by facing his reality, getting input and figuring out a plan of action and getting to work. Many times reality was not pleasant and we were not anxious to help him deal with it. His solutions were not always popular but they were effective.

I remember how Dad used to cut the boys' hair himself so he could save money. He had purchased a clipper and while he knew how to make it work, he was not well schooled in hair styling. Over time and with a few unfortunate mistakes, he mastered the one style that we all came to dislike, the brush cut. At month's end, he would reach over the refrigerator to pull out his clipper. That was the signal for us to run out of the house and hide. We would wait until we thought that Dad was in bed before we came back into the house. Sometimes that strategy worked for us, but there were other times when it did not. Over time Dad figured out what we were up to so he decided to take his clippers and chair outside and keep them hidden. Sometimes he would cut our hair at random times during the month. If we did not come to him, he would come to us. He adapted quickly and, unfortunately for us, he was successful. Once again he faced his reality and got the job done.

Self-fulfilment comes from knowing how your good values and beliefs were acquired and by re-enforcing them, no matter what.

We had a large family so our days were mostly comprised of a family breakfast, lunch, and dinner. The rest of the time we were left to ourselves, spending most of our time seeking new adventures and exploring new experiences. My siblings and I spent a lot of time pushing the boundaries and trying to determine what would keep us out of trouble with Dad and what would result in disciplinary actions. Dad played the role of disciplinarian in the family while Mom was the conciliator. Through trial and error, we quickly learned that some things were non-negotiable. These were the values that would shape us.

- Honesty – always tell the truth.

- Integrity – do what you said you would do.

- Respect – treat others as you would like to be treated.

We made a lot of mistakes growing up and while Dad would cut us some slack on certain things, we could never lie to him. We quickly learned that if we told him the truth, he would show some empathy and ease up on our punishment. While we desperately needed money, he would never let us cheat anyone out of anything. When you worked, you didn't quit at 4:55 ... you never cheat your employer out of the five minutes for which you are getting paid. We all took turns at delivering newspapers on our family paper route and no matter how cold and stormy it was outside, you delivered the paper to the paying customers. You promised the customers a paper everyday, so you had to deliver on that promise. When you submitted the money to the newspaper company, you made sure that there was not a nickel missing. If you would not like to be short-changed by someone, then you should not do it to someone else. He consistently applied the same approach, the same discipline to all of us, every day. No favourites, no shortcuts, no compromises. Period.

Families are stronger than teams. Treat your team as family.

Raising nine children is not an easy task and there were many chores to get done every day. Our parents encouraged (but mostly insisted) that each member of the family pitch in to make the family successful. We all had jobs to do. Some of us cooked, cleaned, and took out the garbage, while others did laundry, dishes, or delivered newspapers around the neighbourhood. Mom and Dad knew that there was no way to keep the family going on their own so, through the delegation of tasks, we were able to contribute in our own unique way which allowed our family to face the daily challenges. While we were all part of the same family, we learned what a team could accomplish when we were made mutually responsible for the overall results and that by supporting each other, we could succeed against all odds. Our family spirit and support for each other would see us through what seemed to be insurmountable odds.

I recall one incident where family teamwork saved my life. After a heavy rain shower, the storm pipe was blocked by debris and the ditch in the front of our house had overflowed. It was quite deep. As the family came home from church, we decided to take a look at the mess.

As I was examining the damage, I slipped and fell into the ditch. I quickly started taking in water and was close to drowning. My family quickly formed a small chain by linking hands and pulled me out to safety. I was quite embarrassed by the incident but also very thankful that my family worked together to pull me to safety. This brought home the point to me that what any one member of my family could not do singly, was made possible when they joined hands as a team.

Courage propels desire into success. Extraordinary people are courageous people with extraordinary goals.

For most of my childhood, Mom was battling cancer. At the time I didn't really understand the severity of her illness. I attribute some of that to my age and lack of maturity, but most of it had to do with the courage that Mom displayed in her fight. If you would have met her for the first time, you would have never known that she was fighting this terrible disease. Despite constant pain, she faced in to the daily tasks of raising our family and was always positive. When she saw us she would light up and, with a warm smile, she greeted us. She catered to our every want, putting our needs ahead of hers. Because of our financial situation, Dad could not afford the time off work to accompany her on her visits to the hospital. We were all in school. She went to hospital by herself for her chemotherapy. While she had periods of remission, over the years she made many visits to the hospital. When I moved to the Toronto area I was able to visit her on a regular basis. Travelling to the hospital was difficult for me. First off, I was afraid to drive into the confusing Toronto downtown area, but mostly I was afraid to face into what I would see when I entered Mom's room. Despite her failing health, she always greeted me the same way, with a warm smile and loving embrace. While she was courageously fighting for her life, she always worried about me. She would say, "I know you're busy so I hope it's not a problem for you to come down here." Somehow she could find the strength to continue to act as a mom instead of a cancer patient. After she finally succumbed to her illness, it struck me that my mother was the most courageous person that I have ever known.

Focus on winning. It's contagious.

Growing up, I saw my dad leave for work by 6:30 a.m every day. In the winter he would brave the cold, sub-zero temperatures where he worked outdoors as a millwright and supervisor at a local sawmill. He would come home for lunch, take a quick nap, and get back to work. He would come back home at 5:15 p.m. for dinner and then he was off to repair things around the house or fix car problems. He usually headed for bed early, but most nights he was summoned from sleep by a call from the nightshift personnel at the mill where old equipment had broken down and they needed Dad to fix it. On weekends he would work all the overtime he could at the sawmill and had taken on side jobs sharpening saws. When the boys in our family reached our teenage years, Dad would get us summer jobs at the sawmill. No matter what I did the night before, Dad would tap me on the shoulder at 6:00 a.m. to get up for work. He could see if I had been out late the night before, laugh at me, and say, If you want to play, you've got to pay. My first experience was piling lumber into stacks eight hours a day in the searing summer heat. It was hard work. I later learned that the reason he made all of us work at the sawmill was not because he wanted us to follow in his footsteps, but he wanted us to know how hard it was to earn a buck. It encouraged us to optimize our education. As he got older, the cold and the hard work were wearing him down. The cold had taken away the feeling in his fingertips and his back needed daily massaging and treatment. Despite all of the personal hardships that he faced, that alarm clock went off every day, and off to work he went. For my eighteen years at home you could set your watch by his punctuality and you could always find him taking his nap at lunch time on the kitchen floor.

If you ask any winning professional athlete, they will tell you that it takes focus and hard work to succeed. That's what my Dad did every day.

These were the values and beliefs that shaped my behaviour. But was I truly following these values in my day to day life as a president? I believed I was in my own way, but the process subsequently helped me understand that not only was I to follow these principles but that I needed to inculcate these principles in each and every member of the organization. That was where the challenge lay. How does one transmit values and inculcate it in a team that is not really a team yet? How do you transfer ownership, accountability, and responsibility to every person in the organization? How do you inspire the team to raise the bar of their performance when they think that they are stretched to the maximum already? I'm sure every leader has asked these questions and has often fumbled with the answers.

There are many books written on this subject and I have read several of them in search of the answer to this question. I have even tried to apply the advice from these books in practice. Somehow I was never satisfied with the outcome.

There are several reasons why it is difficult to apply these concepts in practise:

- A concept is often an ideal, a new approach to doing things, and practical application of an ideal in dealing with people is far from easy.

- Because it is not easy, we seldom follow through.

- Effective application of a concept requires the use of a proven process.

- In order to make the process work, first the leader has to willingly change behaviour and practice what the process preaches.

- The leader must be able to effectively communicate the process and inspire the organization to embrace it.

- The organization must implicitly trust the leader to effectively embrace the process.

- The process must be meticulously tracked.

- The process must provide positive results and feedback.

- The leaders must be prepared to accept and work with honest feedback from the people, good or bad.

- The leaders must become the role models for the process to be cascaded down into the organization.

- There must be effective follow-through throughout the process.

- The leaders must have coaches who keep them on the straight and narrow.

- The whole team must be prepared to make a concerted effort to be mutually responsible and accountable.

- There must be mutual trust and respect at all levels of the organization.

When one reviews the above list, it is not difficult to understand why I found it hard to apply the concepts that one gets in most books on the subject. I feel that the theories in these books are inspirational and innovative, and therefore have always been a source of motivation for me. But when we try to make them work, when the rubber hits the road in business, something seems to snap. One needs to consider all the above points and strictly adhere to them while implementing a new concept to go from being just a good organization to being a great organization.

Unfortunately, once we get into the hustle and bustle of making a business work, the short term pressures take priority and we drop the ball. How many times have you seen a leader come back from a leadership seminar all fired up with a brand new concept that becomes the latest mantra of the day? Everyone repeats it and swears allegiance to it. The concept works wonders for a few weeks and then fades into the background until the leader goes on another leadership seminar and returns with a new mantra.

Lasting change in an organization does not come from motivational phrases or concepts, though they help as a foundation. Lasting change requires that an organization's people change their mindsets and their behaviour to incorporate the change. Given the right process, leadership commitment, people attitudes, and supportive situations, any anticipated change can be incorporated into an organization successfully.

In the following chapter I will describe the prevailing conditions and situations that existed in my organization and the level of change that we wanted to incorporate.

Summary of the Chapter

- Find your teachable point of view and the roots of your values and beliefs.

- Apply your foundational beliefs and values to your day-to-day living.

- The Five Star Power process can be adopted by any leader, no matter what type of organization, because it deals with two common factors that exist in every organization-people and leaders.

- Despite your frustration and your current approach, your company can do well in the short-term and lull you into thinking that you are doing the right thing.

- The process will help you understand that you need to follow your principles and that you need to inculcate these principles in each and every member of the organization.

- Lasting change requires that an organization's people change their mindset and their behaviour to incorporate the change.

Key Message

It's hard to know where you're going if you don't know where you came from.

Chapter Four

Putting Jacques' Philosophy to Work

My career is unique in that I started at the lowest rung of the ladder in The Garland Group and worked my way up to the top job by doing what I believed was the only thing that a leader should do: focus on making things happen. I had limited leadership training and learned on the job, though I did have some good mentors and coaches along the way.

At the time that we introduced the process described in this book, I was facing the following challenges:

I was responsible for a manufacturing business with a factory in Canada and one in the U.S.A along with a Canadian distribution business that represented most of the corporations' products to the Canadian market.

- Reporting to me was a Director of Sales for the Canadian Distribution business who oversaw the sales and marketing. The manufacturing business ran with a functional organization with executives reporting to me who were responsible for finance, sales and marketing, operations and engineering, human resources, parts, and aftermarket service.

- While we were all part of The Garland Group, various sub cultures existed within our company as our distribution business was focused on innovation and customer satisfaction, our Canadian factory was driving operational and process improvements, while our U.S. factory was driving new product introductions.

- It was difficult to create a unified culture given the different cultures (Canada and U.S.A) as well as the different strategies and projects going on in each of the pieces of our business.

- The morale, overall, was low, which was created by a combination of having just come through a tough recession and the conflicting cultures and agendas going on inside our business.

- Historically the employees had got used to working in a top-down management style and had grown comfortable in being told what to do.

- During this time our corporate parent was also undergoing change, which included a name and branding change of the food-service division, along with new centralized organization structure changes within our U.S and international sales teams.

- We were relying heavily on outside recruits to fill key positions as our succession pipeline was weak.

- I was working through my own development and, as a Canadian based executive with a U.S. parent, I found myself needing to take personal responsibility for my development

Therefore I faced the following challenges:

- I was dealing with a distinct culture and management style in the U.S..

- A distinct culture and management style in Canada.

- A distinct culture and management style at the corporate office.

- A distinct culture and management style when dealing with the global entities.

- I needed to integrate the above cultures and styles and build a cohesive team.

- I needed to improve the morale and create a meaningful vision that would inspire the team.

- I needed to have people embrace change.

- I needed to personally develop my leadership skills and those of my leaders.

Accordingly I decided to address FIVE issues head on:

- As the leader and the organization as a whole I needed to face the reality of our current situation.

- Having done that, we needed to develop a vision that every individual in the organization could understand and own.

- We needed to integrate the various cultures and create a mutually supportive team.

- We needed to create a more disciplined culture that recognized and worked with accountability and responsibility.

- We needed to have the leaders lead at all levels of the organization.

How I Got There

I made my way through grade and high school focusing primarily on sports and maintaining good grades. I attended community college in North Bay and graduated with my diploma in business administration. In January 1985 I launched into my professional career with my first full time job as Internal Sales Clerk at Garland in Mississauga, Canada.

Early in my career, I relied mostly on hard work and my intuition and I was getting good results. As I would come to learn later in life, I was "hard wired" with strong strategic and tactical reasoning skills. My efforts were being recognized by customers, peers, and the senior management team.

I was quickly promoted to supervisor where my journey into leadership began. That is where I entered the world of self-improvement and started searching for ways to become more effective as a leader. I read many books to benchmark other leaders and studied change management. While I gained much insight and made incremental improvements, I did not find any breakthroughs. While I was getting good results and was getting promoted, I found that I had to work harder and harder. I was getting worn out and my family life was starting to suffer.

My career path led to a Vice President of Sales role and then as General Manager, I moved into my first manufacturing assignment. While my responsibility grew, I continued to deliberately educate myself in the technical elements that I needed to succeed in my job but my leadership skills were not keeping pace. So I had to bridge the gap with more hard work, longer hours, and cancelled vacations. This was all taking a deeper toll on my family. Meanwhile, the president was pushing me for results.

In the fall of 2000, I was promoted to Group President. It was both exciting and scary. I was now responsible for a distribution company and two factories that designed, manufactured, and sold products into a hundred countries. While I had gained much experience and brought capability to the job, I knew that my workload was going to increase and that for me to succeed in this assignment, I would have to grow. The question was, how?

After working long hours and many seven day work weeks, I knew that I was operating at a pace that was not sustainable. In 2002 our business was improving and we were growing. While sales grew under 1%, we managed a 45% increase in profit. In 2003, sales grew again and profit improved by another 50%. During that time we continued to grow our talent, improve our execution, and tighten up our efficiencies. I was still working very long hours, leaving little time for my personal life.

While we were performing well, our results were underpinned by almost super human effort. I had accomplished this by micro-managing and was undermining my managers and under-utilizing their skills and capabilities. I was tired and spending too few hours at home with my family.

No one was celebrating. Morale was low and our employee surveys highlighted a lack of trust in management. Our company lacked the speed and flexibility which I felt we needed to compete and win in the future. While nobody was coming up to me and saying it, we all knew that something was missing and that we were not performing at our peak capacity. I was worried that we were headed for trouble and spent many sleepless nights thinking about how I could get more out of the team.

I knew that we needed a fresh approach, but what? I was awfully lonely at the top!

I started talking to friends and colleagues. A long-time coach suggested I meet with Carl Phillips. We met at my office one day where Carl introduced me to the notion that people manage reality if you lead them. This struck a chord with me since it was aligned with my childhood experience and beliefs. While I did not fully understand what I was about to do and that most of the change that had to take place had to do with my leadership abilities, I shook hands with Carl and we got down to work.

In the four years following, our sales growth accelerated to over 11% per year, reaching 19% in 2008, and our earnings more than doubled to record levels. We had a new and inspiring vision for the future and were working as a team to realize it. Morale had improved to record levels and people were taking the initiative across the company. Cross functional, self-directed work teams were driving change in our company and customer satisfaction surveys showed dramatic improvement. The Garland Group employees had become a team. We were adept at facing reality, making decisions around it, and quickly "getting on with it". I knew that we had something special.

In the following chapters we will detail how we did it, how we emphasized an integrated drive on dynamics and mechanics, and how we applied the Five Star Power process to achieve breakthrough results.

Summary of the Chapter

- As the leader, I needed to face the reality of our current situation and take action.

- Working long hours and seven day work weeks is operating at a pace that is not sustainable.

- Your team will sense that they are not performing at their peak capacity, but may not say anything or have any opinions on what needs to be done.

- No matter how hard you work, there are only so many hours in the day and only so much that you can do.

- You have an organization for a definite reason and that is for you to effectively use all the power that you have.

- I had potential leaders but they were under-utilized and were often waiting for direction from me to take the initiative.

- We needed help as an organization and were not afraid to seek it.

- Emphasizing an integrated drive on dynamics and applying the Five Star Power process achieved breakthrough results and continues to do so. It can do the same for you.

Key Message

If you want to win, sustain your performance over the long term and keep the balance in your life. Don't be lonely at the top.

Chapter Five

Five Star Power: The Power of People Dynamics for Your Organization

Every person in an organization has individual perceptions and expectations of every event that occurs in the organization. These perceptions comprise the beliefs of the individual about the person's job. That individual tends to implement jobs at work based on these expectations. If they believe that only customers should be treated courteously, then they will only treat outside customers courteously and take their colleagues for granted with limited attention to courtesy. How do you think that person's colleagues react to this behaviour? Obviously they will react in kind. If this is so, do you then think that this behaviour is conducive to building a mutually supportive team in such a group? What about the loss of productivity as a result? You are now dealing with people dynamics.

Throughout my career as a consultant, I have asked the same question, "Who do you consider a customer?" I have never got the response that everyone in the organization is a customer. The thesaurus defines a customer as a supporter or a patron. I would think every person in the organization is a supporter of everyone else in the organization. It is not commonly accepted that every person in an organization is a customer. The word customer is commonly taken to mean clients of the organization or outside clients, not internal clients. Though it is not hard to visualize the fact that everyone in an organization supports everyone else and therefore internal people are customers of each other.

It helps people in an organization to treat each other with the respect and courtesy that they reserve normally only for customers. Why do they need this reminder? Isadore Sharp explains this very succinctly. Isadore Sharp, founder, chairman, and CEO of the Four Seasons Hotels and Resorts, put Canadian five star hotels on the world map. I have personally visited more than fifty countries and I always stayed in a Four Seasons hotel if there was one in the place I was visiting. The reason for this is simple. I always received top class personalized service in these hotels. What made these hotels different?

One has to read Sharp's business philosophy to understand why these hotels were different. In his book *Four Seasons, the Story of a Business Philosophy*, Sharp reaffirms his belief that every employee should be treated as a customer in order for the employee to treat their customers right. This is the secret weapon of the Four Seasons hotel chain.

Sharp's philosophy was not out of a book. It was a common sense statement of a fact. It was an assertion made by a grass roots individual of the reality of leading people. He instinctively understood and applied people dynamics to the leading of people. Sharp gets it.

If you want to raise the productivity and general morale of your organization, you have to create a culture that is people dynamics conscious. You will then experience the thrill of leading an organization that functions at the five star level.

So why do I compare a five star rating to the rating of leadership? The major difference in a two star hotel and a five star hotel is the quality of personalized service. The difference in a poor business leader and a great business leader is also the leader's ability to engender a personalized service culture. You pay more money, you normally get better amenities. You pay more money and it does not necessarily follow that you will get better service, though one is often led to believe that this is so. In any case, the quality of amenities and service is the basis for rating hotels from one to five.

The quality of amenities is readily visible. On the other hand, the quality of service is somewhat more subtle, though a much more powerful measure. If your leadership was rated on your ability to inculcate service in your employees, what rating do you think you would get from your employees? Would you be a five star or a two star leader? It may surprise you how your employees rate you and how you rate yourself.

In the previous chapter, Jacques Seguin started out to be a five star leader. The rating of five is normally viewed as a top rating. Hotels are rated as five stars because of their top level of service. In the armed forces, the top of the leadership ladder is a five star general. The five star concept seems to generate an image of top quality leadership performance.

In order for a leader to perform at a five star level, there are five critical steps that we have to follow in sequence. We have termed these steps 'stars'. Each star has to be earned by a leader before moving on to the next star. A star cannot be effectively attempted unless the previous star has been achieved; this is a progressive process.

Jacques Seguin's focus was to follow the five star processes enumerated in the first chapter in order to become a five star leader. As we follow Jacques' quest, we will first outline what should be done by the leader and then Jacques will enumerate how this played out in the organization, giving us both the positive outcomes and the negative fallout from the achievement of actions given in each star. In essence, we will give you the proven process first, and Jacques will then outline the practical implications and challenges that one has to face while implementing the process. Hopefully you will have the detailed process with its practical implications through this approach so that it can serve as a do-it-yourself tool.

Bear in mind that Jacques had to implement the process while exercising his personal understanding and acceptance of the management of reality in the work environment. He had to draw on his experience and embedded people skills to implement a process that challenged his beliefs and values. Even as he implemented the process, he had to change his influencing skills, believing in the validity and reliability of the process, despite considerable scepticism in his employees. Though he seldom wavered in his resolve to follow through, he would have to draw on all his internal reserves to soldier on. As you read on, you must be aware that being a five star leader is not for the faint of heart.

To become a five star leader, one has to meticulously follow the five star processes in the sequence given below:

- Start operating in the real world personally.

- Target the common vision and engender commitment to it.

- Assemble mutually supportive teams.

- Reward a disciplined culture.

- Seed and seek innovative leaders at all levels.

The Five Star Power process is the gateway to a leader's development in managing reality. In order to help others focus on the difficult task of identifying, accepting, and dealing effectively with reality, one needs to follow a proven process in a disciplined and persistent manner starting with the leader's personal attitude to reality. The leader sets the example for the rest of the organization.

Many leaders understand very clearly what the above statement means and accept the fact that the leader's behaviour sets the standard for the rest of the organization. However, when it comes to the leader changing personal behaviour first before demanding that same behaviour change from others, only a handful of leaders do. This is not often the fault of leadership *per se*. Most leaders have followed a common misunderstood concept of leadership-that of motivating people through the carrot or the stick.

So the first star that the leader has to earn before attempting to lead people is to recognize, accept, and personally adjust to the evolving reality that people need to be respected and treated as owners of the business before they will behave like owners. In essence, the leader has to evaluate their personal operating style to accommodate this perspective, and based on the leader's findings, reorient the operating style, no matter how painful it may be to do so.

A glaring example of leadership behaviour that did not acknowledge the evolving reality was provided during the global financial crisis of 2008 by the executives of large financial institutions in the United States. They were happily walking away with large bonuses while the organizations were on the verge of going bankrupt. Were those executives personally facing reality and setting an example for others? Were they walking the talk? With this standard of leadership, is it any wonder that the organizations in question were in trouble?

This star is one of the hardest to achieve because it often goes against the grain of traditional human reaction to bad news. Like the proverbial ostrich we find it easier to hide our heads in the sand rather than face the reality of bad news. How often have we sat at a meeting and knowingly heard someone sugarcoat a situation and said nothing to set the record straight?

Do you know why? Clearly it is because we do not want to be seen as the bad news bearer or worse still, sound negative or cynical. Incidentally, people who behave like that at meetings are killing the organization with what they would see as kindness or as being a good team player.

Reality does not respect politeness or kindness. It is what it is. Period. A true team player feels mutually responsible in a group meeting and expects to be respected for exposing the reality of the situation and thereby averting a future crisis for the team. The most effective way for a leader to draw attention to reality is to change the leader's behaviour to effectively reflect the reality. For instance, if the organization does not understand the concept that treating the internal customers well sets the stage for the internal customers to treat the external customers even better, the leader models the correct behaviour first. With this in mind, the next chapter launches the first star of the Five Star process.

Summary of the Chapter

- Every person in an organization is a customer.

- Isadore Sharp says that if we want our employees to treat our customers right, we must treat our employees as customers.

- People need to be treated as owners before they behave like owners.

- A great business leader is able to engender a personalized service culture in an organization, so that every person in the organization is treated as a customer.

- The first is the toughest star to achieve by a leader because the leader has to personally change to face the reality demanded by the change.

- We are what we do, not what we say.

- We must face reality when functioning in a team, not avoid it and feel you are being a team player by being polite and kind.

- Reality does not respect politeness or kindness. It is what it is. Period.

- We need to have the courage of our convictions and stand up and be counted to be able to help an organization face reality.

Key Message

People behave the way they are treated, not the way they are told to behave.

Chapter Six

The First Leadership Star
(S t a r s)
Start Operating in the Real World

"We must become the change we want to see." Mahatma Gandhi

Truer words were never spoken as it relates to leaders. At the same time, nothing can be more difficult to implement. One of the hidden motives for leaders to be in-charge of things is for them to be able to tell others what to do and supervise them. In fact, the reward for doing a good job as an individual is to be given the prize position of supervising others. Of course, supervisors like parents learn to their dismay that people do not do what you tell them to do. Instead, they do what you do. That is the real world. So the first step in setting an organization on the straight and narrow is for the leader to start operating in the real world by modelling the way. How do we do this?

We implement the first star of the FIVE STAR POWER process. The first step requires that we find a way to provide the leader with a wake-up call to the realities that exist in the organization and the real impact that the leader has on the organization. We need to help the leader to deal honestly with these realities that are either ignored or glossed over or are unrecognized. We do this by using a modified version of the 360 degree feedback process in conjunction with a personal development procedure for the leader. The start of the process requires the leader to fill out a questionnaire, as honestly and realistically as it can be done. See Appendix A. Once this is done, a similar questionnaire in Appendix B is given to:

- The leader's direct reports.

- A few respected leaders lower down in the organization.

- The leader's colleagues.

- The leader's boss.

- A few select customers.

- A few select suppliers.

For this stage, it would be ideal for the leader to have a mentor who can assist the leader in objectively gathering the information required. In our case, I (Carl Phillips) was responsible for the collection and collation of the information for Jacques. This provided an opportunity for Jacques to face the brutal facts of the obstacles that existed in reality in his organization, whether it is behaviour, values, or process related.

The Process

In the first step of the process, we had to establish how Jacques saw himself and what his driving forces were. In order to do this, a customized questionnaire was prepared for him to answer. Once he had filled out the questionnaire, I interviewed him to clarify and at times challenge his thoughts. This then provided a base for me to compare his thoughts with the thoughts of others who interfaced with him on a day-to-day basis. The gap in these findings would reveal the realities that Jacques needed to understand, accept, and effectively deal with. More importantly, Jacques needed to understand the dynamics that were released when he communicated to the organization, how the organization interpreted his behaviour, and how they were reacting to what they interpreted as Jacques' intentions. He needed to understand how he influenced the thinking and behaviour of the people of the organization. In other words, he had to internalize the fact that his behaviour was the main influence on the behaviour of the people of the organization. Having understood the difference in his perception of himself and that of the people he interfaced with on a regular basis, and the need for him to re-orientate his behaviour, he had to accept it and then commit to an action plan to change accordingly. Then he had to implement that plan.

For example, Jacques was perceived as a formal person who was difficult to approach in informal settings. Jacques is a genuine individual and what you see is what you get, but he was obviously projecting a formal image without really knowing the impact he was having on the senior team and subsequently on the effectiveness of his organization. More importantly, he was modelling the behaviour that senior team members emulated and accordingly were unconsciously transmitting the message that this was the culture of the company. It is not rocket science to figure out how this culture can hinder the effective functioning of an organization. It is important to understand who sets the pattern of behaviour for the organization and what impact that behaviour can have on the performance of the company. It all starts with the leader.

There are many books written on culture and how it is embedded in an organization, so this is not a platform for that discussion. However, when I ran my own company, I once requested a new hire to do something for me. Not knowing who I was, she said to me that she could not do it because she was told that Carl did not like it! To which I said, "Hi, I'm Carl, and let me tell you that I like it." Someone had decided the way to do that particular job and had added my name as the authority. Even worse, someone had taken my instructions and misinterpreted them to embed a process that was not in sync with the stated values of the organization. In a formal culture, this discrepancy would not ordinarily surface, leading to the wrong culture being embedded.

As I interviewed Jacques against the questionnaire at Appendix A, I was developing a profile of Jacques as he saw himself, including his personal vision, his values, and his behaviours. I then interviewed the people enumerated above against the questionnaire at Appendix B to get their perception of Jacques' vision, values, and behaviours. These two different perspectives provided the basis for the implementation of the Five Star processes;

- Start operating in the real world—Jacques' personal development.

- Target the common vision—the creation of a common vision.

- Assemble mutually supportive teams—organization team building.

- Reward a disciplined culture—embed a new, effective culture.

- Seed and seek leaders at all levels of the organization.

Jacques followed this process meticulously, and the company continues to reap the rewards from his ongoing efforts to truly embed all the above changes.

Twenty Questions for Leadership Self Analysis

(Appendix A)

This questionnaire is specifically designed to identify your needs, and your personal and business goals in order to help you lead a great organization. The questions are meant to trigger an introspective personal review of the philosophies that drive a leader's actions and help shape a person's basic beliefs and values. It is suggested that you take a moment and search your thoughts critically and objectively even though you might hesitate to admit them. Remember, what got you and your organization to your current level of performance, no matter how good, will not get you to the next level. You have to develop your personal performance level to raise the level of the organization and thus set the standard for the people of the organization. The organization cannot rise above the level of the leadership that it is provided. Put more bluntly, If you want to raise the performance of your organization by 25%, then you have to raise your leadership level at least by 25%!

This questionnaire provides you the platform to be brutally honest about your needs to raise your personal bar of performance as you perceive them. Please respond to these questions with this in mind. Because each question may prompt different lengths of response, please answer the questions on separate sheets of paper.

1. Take a moment to reflect on the question, "Who am I?" Define yourself as an individual as you see yourself and not as you believe others see you.

2. Answer the question, "What am I?"

   - Describe three key abilities.

   - Describe three areas of deep interest that you enjoy.

   - Describe three areas of development that you feel you need.

3. Describe three critical incidents in your life that are difficult to forget:

   - Why was each incident critical for you?

   - What positive growth did each incident trigger in your life?

4. What are your personal goals in the:

   - Long Term (Five Years)?

   - Midterm (Three years)?

   - Short Term (One Year)?

5. What are your business goals in the:

- Long Term (Five Years)?

- Midterm (Three Years)?

- Short Term (One Year)?

6. Are your personal goals in sync with your business goals? If they are not in sync, how do you plan to integrate the two?

7. How will you know when you have achieved each of the above goals:

8. What type of support would you like to get to achieve these goals from:

- Your boss or bosses.

- Your colleagues.

- Your direct reports.

- Your customers, internal and external.

- Your suppliers.

- Your coach or mentor.

9. What are the three most critical aspects of your current operating style that you know that you have to change in order for you to achieve these goals?

10. Do you seek feedback from the people mentioned in question #8? If so, how does their feedback differ from your perception of yourself?

11. Name three actions that you need to take in order to inspire your organization onto greater achievements.

12. It has been seen that people who believe in the vision of a company perform at least 30% more effectively than those who are less committed to the vision. How will you get your people to believe in the vision?

13. Does your executive team believe in the following rules of engagement of a team?

    - Knowing each other well enough to be able to leverage each other's strengths and support each other's weaknesses?

    - Having common goals?

    - Having a common approach to achieve these goals?

    - Having a common measure of success for these goals?

    - Being mutually accountable and supportive for the achievement of these goals.?

If not, how do you plan to embed these rules of engagement for teams in your organization?

14. Do you believe that the purpose of leadership is to create more leaders? If you do, then how would you plan to inculcate this concept in your organization when:

    - Recruiting new hires?

    - Mentoring and coaching?

    - Supervising and managing?

- Career planning and succession planning?

- Promoting?

- Innovating?

- Rewarding?

15. What are the top three values that you would like the organization to excel at?

16. How would you embed these values in your organization?

17. In order to compete effectively at the global level, you need to create a new exciting culture in your organization that is disciplined, informed, agile and innovative. How would you do this?

18. When given a goal, do you believe that failure is not an option? If you do, then you need to do something that will reinforce this concept within the next three months. State that action as a personal commitment.

19. Given that the operating styles of leaders have to quickly adapt to the changing face of business, what changes in your behaviour are required to adapt to the following changes in the business world:

- Globalization.

- Leadership.

- Communication.

- Innovation.

- Transparency.

- Quality.

20. There is a saying that, "You cannot be promoted if you cannot be replaced." How have you tackled this issue in your own case? Also, how have you tackled this issue in the organization as a whole?

Most leaders when answering this questionnaire find that they come face to face with a host of subjects connected with their personal goals and ambitions and their own operating styles that forces them to rethink their role as a leader of an organization. They are then often prepared to reset their personal plans for themselves and for the organization as a whole.

In the following chapter, Jacques will outline his experiences with the process and how it helped him reset his own goals.

Summary of the Chapter

- Leaders get promoted into management positions because they perform well as individuals.

- Leaders as managers learn fast that people do not do what you tell them to do, they do what you do, based on their perceptions of you.

- Leaders need to change their behaviour if they want others to change.

- The first star is the most difficult star for a leader to achieve.

- The leader needs a wake-up call to reality.

- The process compares how the leader sees him or her and how the leader thinks the organization sees them. The gap in these two perspectives defines the developmental needs of the leader.

- The leader's behaviour dictates the corporate values and culture.

- A detailed twenty question questionnaire for leadership self-analysis is included.

Key Message

Perception is reality. Leaders need to deal with the perceptions of people in order to deal with their realities.

Chapter Seven

Evaluating the Leader's Perception of Reality

As Carl mentioned in chapter 6, the FIVE STAR POWER process begins by starting to operate in the real world and facing reality. As Carl took me through this step, I wrestled with this both intellectually and emotionally. On the intellectual side, I thought, "what could be so tough about operating in the real world?" While we live in a dynamic global world, surely I was smart enough to figure out what reality was. After all, there are plenty of newspapers, books, and people to talk to. There are plenty of sources of data. I knew how to access that information and was making good use of it in my planning and decision making. Why then was I not operating in the real world? As I started to shift my focus to my emotions I found that with operating in the real world came fear.

As I continued to dig deeper inside, I found that fear, not the lack of the understanding of reality, was in fact the largest barrier in facing my reality. When you face reality, you have nowhere to go but to deal with it. For example, there were leaders who were extremely smart and hard working, but I had promoted them into the wrong slot. Facing this reality meant that I had to do something to change their roles and risk generating an atmosphere of uncertainty in the organization. What would be the accompanying organization dynamics? What would the cost of this change be? Where would I put them so that they would continue to be motivated and committed? The fear of this risk, and the fact that I was not sure how they would react, made me hesitate. The longer I procrastinated, the more the performance of the company suffered. I believe that the reality that something had to change was palpable throughout the organization. The moment I faced this reality head on, the solution became evident and there was an unheard sigh of relief in the leadership of the organization. More importantly, I believe by me facing the reality, other leaders of the organization were encouraged to do the same and thus pick up the pace of decision making.

So how do I overcome this fear to deal with the real issues and take action against the issues and opportunities that comprise our reality? This is where Carl's questionnaire effectively uncovered the source of the fear as well as the source of the courage that I would need to start operating in the real world. Also, it made me face the most brutal reality, which is that I had to internalize the fact that my behaviour was the main influence on others. If I wanted to change the behaviour of others, I would need to change my behaviour first. This brings up another type of fear: the fear of the unknown. If I changed my behaviour, I would have to operate outside my comfort zone, and I was not sure that I was that eager to face up to the consequences. The other guys were not the problem; I was. As these questions will be challenging for you, I will take you through my thoughts and feelings, as I worked through the questions.

Questions 1, 2 and 3. When Carl first asked me to answer these questions, I did a superficial scan of my skills and came up with a summary of feedback that I had received from others over time. Carl kept pushing me on this issue: "Jacques, this is not the real you, take a deeper look inside." This started to raise some doubts in my mind which led me to the conclusion that I had never really taken the time to take a hard look at myself. What are my beliefs and values? What do I believe in? How do I behave and why? Most importantly, what were the events that shaped these in me? This is about getting in touch with who you are and why. As I peeled back the layers, I was suddenly able to understand myself better and connect the events that shaped me since my childhood. Going through this process had a very calming effect on me as I gained a much deeper understanding of myself. I felt grounded for the first time in my life. My outline is captured in chapter 3 of the book. I suggest that you go back to review that chapter as a suggested road map for you to take in answering the first three questions.

Questions 4, 5 ,6, 7 and 8. These questions caused me to shift from an introspective mindset to thinking about what I was trying to achieve. I quickly concluded that, while I had used goal setting over the years, I had been inconsistent at best and that my goal setting was mainly focused on professional goals. I had not set personal goals for myself. Personal goals like improving my fitness, being a better husband or father, spending more time helping others or just taking a vacation to recoup. In essence, by not setting goals I was not providing the inspiration that I needed to drive me to reach a new level of performance, which I knew would be needed if my team and company were to reach the next level of performance. I was basically just doing my job as well as I could but was not feeling fully satisfied and fulfilled. I needed to have both the personal and professional goals to be in sync to drive me and that one without the other, would not work. How many great leaders do you know that are terrible people? To be a great leader, you need to be a great person. Great people are able to balance their personal and their professional lives. To this day I can still remember the feeling of pride as I crossed the finish line as I completed a half marathon.

Having a goal, working towards it, achieving that goal, and most importantly, celebrating yourself are critical elements on the journey towards peak performance. When is the last time that you celebrated yourself as you achieved one of your goals? As you work through question eight, you will learn to include others in the development and support of your goal setting and achievement. As I learned, your friends and coworkers can help you if you choose to include them. When I tell my assistant that I have a goal to run a marathon, she will help me keep on track by reminding me of the need for me to keep in shape and allow training time in my schedule.

After completing questions one through eight, I came to a sobering realization that I had spent a significant portion of my life without a deep understanding of who I was. I was wandering around aimlessly hoping that success and happiness would find me. This had to change and I was going to make it happen.

Questions 9 through 12. This is where I started to shape the changes that I needed to make. Based on a deeper understanding of myself, I now had increased confidence and new found courage to start making changes. But it was still tough. This is where working out the differences between my desired operating style and my perceived operating style was critical. And having the confidence to ask your team for honest feedback through a 360 feedback exercise is critical. Having completed a few of these exercises since my first one with Carl, there is always a gap in how you think you are leading and how it is being perceived by your team. You have all heard the saying, "it's lonely at the top," but I learned that it does not have to be that way. I could include others with my development and others were keenly interested in my development and my success. You just have to ask.

As I now started setting integrated personal and professional goals, I was feeling energized and inspired. This energy was starting to transfer to my team. As I worked through question eleven, I searched for the definition of inspiration and settled on "connecting a person's actions to a goal that they perceive to be worthwhile". That's how I defined inspiration. While I had created goals for myself, I needed to set inspirational goals for my company. This meant the creation of a vision that was inspiring and meaningful to every person in the organization. Further on in future chapters, I will talk about the creation of such a vision.

Questions 13 to 18. Setting the standard for values and behaviours. As I started to modify my behaviours, I knew that this would impact the behaviour of others. Aligning their behaviour modifications to my desired end state, required creating and articulating the accepted standard for our company values and behaviours. This required much work and many hours working with the senior team to gain agreement. From there we talked through each of the elements and set expectations for modelling the behaviour.

Through my example, an expectation was set for my team that they also had to be teachable and that they not only had to improve their leadership style, they had to develop new leaders. This had a cascading effect on all levels of our organization and introduced new people practices into our company such as coaching, mentoring, succession planning, and behavioural interviewing. I was starting to see the logic behind the saying "a company cannot outgrow the capabilities of its people".

Questions 19 and 20. These prepare you to break out of the paradigm. To think big and to prepare yourself personally to take the next step in your performance and career.

Answering this questionnaire did several things for me. I was forced to be honest with myself about what was my self image. How did I develop it, where was I headed in life, and what did I want to have when I got there? More importantly, I was opening up myself to change. I was beginning to stagnate and because of my previous success, feel that I had arrived as a president and therefore needed little further development as a leader. Of course I expected to keep polishing up my skills, but not anything as deep as to re-value my basic beliefs and behaviours.

I had done a 360 degree feedback exercise before, but more often than not I treated it as getting feedback from my colleagues as to how they perceived me. This often left it open for me to accept their perceptions as correct or to tell myself that their perceptions were wrong because they may have misread my intentions. On the other hand, for the first time I was facing the fact that how my colleagues perceived me was mostly dependent on how I behaved toward them, irrespective of my intentions. In other words, I was responsible for the perception of my colleagues and therefore I could change their perceptions or even dictate their perceptions. My good intentions would not be considered unless they were clearly reflected in my behaviour towards others. All of a sudden it began to dawn on me that not only did I have to understand myself as a person, but I also had the responsibility as a leader for shaping the behaviour of the leaders of the organization through the shaping of my own behaviour! I would be perceived the way I wanted others to perceive me. More importantly, if I wanted to raise the capability of the leaders of the organization I would have to first raise my own capability and then through my behaviour inspire others to raise their capability.

These thoughts put a premium on my thinking as to the importance of my day-to-day behaviour whether it is as a leader, a parent, or a member of society. I was being perceived as I behaved, and people treated me the way they perceived me. If I was not being treated right then I had only myself to blame. If as a leader I was not being effective, then I only had myself to blame. I could not blame the economic climate, the other leaders or the markets. If I was not effective as a leader, it meant that I was not adapting my behaviour effectively and getting others to do the same. Of course, there is such a thing as bad luck and unforeseen circumstances that often intervene and disrupt one's efforts, but that would be out of my sphere of influence. I am addressing the main issues that a leader can and should influence in an organization through behaviour alone. You will be surprised how lucky you, your team and your organization can get when you are displaying the right behaviour. In fact, behaviour subtly drives or represses performance as you will see as you read further.

Summary of the Chapter

- Part of "operating in the real world" is fear.

- For when you face reality, you have nowhere to go but to deal with it.

- The longer you procrastinate, the more the performance of the company suffers.

- When the leader faces reality, other leaders of the organization are encouraged to do the same and thus pick up the pace of decision making.

- If the leader changes their behaviour, they have to operate outside their comfort zone so they are not always eager to face up to the consequences.

- Through example, an expectation is set amongst the team that they also have to be teachable and that they, not only have to improve their leadership style, they have to develop new leaders.

- You are responsible for the perception of your colleagues and therefore, you can change their perceptions or even dictate their perceptions. Your good intentions would not be considered unless they were clearly reflected in your behaviour towards them.

Key Message

If there's a problem, the leader should take immediate responsibility. The other leaders are not the problem, you are. The way to change their behavior is by changing yours.

Chapter Eight

The Leader's Behaviour Defines
the Corporate Values

Before you become a leader, you are responsible for your own behaviour. When you become a leader, your behaviour becomes the beacon and guiding framework for the organization that you lead. Your words, passionate speeches, and upbeat emails create the initial inspiration and excitement which quickly fades if you do not personally follow through with the behaviour that corresponds to those words. You must walk your talk. Your exceptionally good behaviour as a leader is the fountainhead for sustained high level performance in an organization. People do what you do, not what you tell them to do.

Dennis Eck was the Managing Director and CEO of Coles Meyer, Australia's largest retail chain with approximately 180,000 employees, and annual sales of $20 billion . I interviewed him for my book *Global Literacies*. Dennis took over the company after it had been through a few very rough years. One of the main reasons for their loss of market share Dennis decided was that they had forgotten how to treat customers well. He wanted to help them change their behaviour towards their customers. So Dennis installed video cameras in front of the customer service desks in each store. The cameras were trained on the customers as they approached the customer service desks. After a day's work, Dennis suggested that each customer service person should watch the tape and study the expressions and actions of each customer as the customer service person dealt with the customer. This exercise helped the customer service persons to see what impact their behaviour had on the customer. If they were abrupt and curt with the customer, the customer behaved in a similar manner. If, on the other hand, they were polite and cordial with the customer, they found that the customers were polite and cordial in their responses. This exercise was very effective in bringing home the point that the customer service person could control the behaviour of the customer. As Dennis expanded on these findings, he was able to change the behaviour of the people towards customer relations in Coles Meyer, and accordingly raise the company profile to the leading retail chain in Australia and New Zealand.

You are not what you think you are as a leader, but what others think of you. This does not mean that your perceptions of yourself are wrong or that you should let others dictate your standards and values. It often does not matter what you think of yourself as a leader when it comes to managing people. It just means that people behave towards you based on how they perceive your behaviour. Their perception becomes their reality. Your perception of yourself has a built-in self-justification for any deviant behaviour, and more often than not, you see your behaviour through rose tinted glasses that make you look good. Others do not have any built-in justification for your behaviour and therefore they define your raw behaviour as an expression of your fixed personality. It is quite possible that your perceived image may not be your true image as you see it, but your image of yourself does not dictate how people will behave towards you. I am often surprised by how someone defines my intentions based on my behaviour. No matter how much I protest or try to justify my actions, it is very hard to erase the distorted perception as I see it. On reviewing my behaviour, I could understand why I gave the opposite impression of my intentions, while being oblivious of its impact. I felt that my good intentions would be understood and therefore, when read in conjunction with my behaviour, it would have an overall favourable impression.

Unfortunately, this is often not so. Think of the employer who feels justified in letting an underperforming employee go. The employer is often disappointed and sorry for the employee but feels justified and fair in taking the action. Then think of the underperforming employee's perception of the employer's behaviour. Very often the employee will feel very hard done by and would not accept the employer's behaviour as justified. In fact, the employee might go so far as to think of the employer as unfair and prejudiced. I do not mean to imply that either person is wrong in their perceptions. The message here is that in these very complex situations there is a definite need for detailed dialogue, sensitivity, and appropriate preparation before such extreme action as letting a person go is taken. Otherwise the fallout can sometimes be disastrous as we know from experience. It is commonly known that the US Postal Service has had at least twenty incidents between 1986 and 1997 in which forty people were gunned down by previously fired postal workers. In fact, "going postal" in American English slang means becoming extremely and uncontrollably angry, often to the point of violence, usually in a workplace environment.

More importantly, what others think of your behaviour as a leader towards them becomes their frame of reference for their behaviour. How many times have you walked into a company and the cheerful atmosphere of the company offices strikes you as reflective of the behaviour of the leaders of those offices? On the other hand, you can walk into a company that has a very serious and sober bunch of leaders and more often than not you will be able to hear a pin drop and it will feel like it would be a sin that is punishable by death if you so much as attempt to crack a joke. I once had a client in the UK. My earliest impression of him was through my contacts with his assistant. She was a status-conscious person who would not talk to my assistant, but demanded to speak directly to me for details. She was also very abrupt and unfriendly on the phone. When I eventually met up with the CEO of this assistant, it was like I was talking to his assistant. His behaviour was almost identical to his assistant's. She was emulating his behaviour as the standard.

It is not uncommon for a leader to believe that corporate values and standards are developed by the leader taking a lot of pains to clarify them. They often believe that the following actions will embed corporate behaviour in an organization:

- Getting agreement by the leaders on the values and behaviours in an extensive off-site meeting.

- Distributing booklets clarifying the same in detail.

- Even having the values printed on the back of every person's personal business card.

- Constantly having them repeat these values till they know them by heart.

Time and again I have seen that these actions do not dictate the behaviours, though they do provide a good point of reference. On numerous occasions I have confronted senior leaders of organizations as to their corporate values, and more often than not they have rattled them off by heart. Yet their colleagues and their team members would have given me feedback earlier that their performance as leaders was lacking in those same values.

As leaders, your behaviour sets the framework for the behaviour of others in the organization. It is almost independent of what you lay down as the preferred behaviour for the organization in the form of company values and standards; your behaviour sets the standard. In fact, if you feel that people are not treating your customers right, examine your own behaviour, and nine out of ten times you will find that your behaviour triggered the undesirable behaviour of others. Just try this experiment to see this concept in action:

At an organization social gathering be very reserved and aloof as the leader. You will notice that others will also be reserved and aloof towards you. On the other hand, if you are outgoing and friendly with everybody, you will suddenly find that people will be outgoing and friendly towards you. You dictate the way people behave towards you. Therefore, the concept that follows is that in order to change the behaviour of others, you must change your own behaviour towards them first. This is why most leaders hesitate to make required changes in an organization: they know instinctively that they will have to change personally first before they demand that others change.

If I were to name the single most misunderstood concept in leadership, it would be the fact that most leaders believe that if they have good overall intentions in instituting a particular change, that the change will be perceived as positive. The fact that the leader's behaviour is often out of sync with the stated change, resulting in an overall negative perception of the change, is a complete blind spot for the leader. In other words, there are those who believe that a leader's actions are not that important, if the leader has good intentions. How leaders perceive their own behaviour is seen as the only important issue for the leader, when the only issue of major importance is how those who are led perceive the leader's actions. Companies have paid the ultimate price in their fields because the leaders of the company have not quite internalized this concept. Let me give you a real life example of this phenomenon.

I was involved in a feedback session of a vice president of a company. The feedback was being given by the president, who did a good job of being very balanced in the process. One of the issues that the president gave to the vice president was that even though the VP was a good conscientious worker, he tended to make it difficult to manage him because the VP always seemed to disagree with any feedback that he was given. At this point the VP vehemently disagreed with the president, saying that on the contrary, he was very amenable to feedback, not recognizing the fact that he had just proved the president right. The president just smiled and said, "You may be correct in your statement based on how you perceive your own behaviour, but my feedback is about how I perceive your behaviour. Unfortunately, my behaviour towards you is dictated by the way I perceive your behaviour and not how you perceive your own behaviour. On the other hand, if you are so confident about your own behaviour, then just help me change my perception." The penny dropped immediately for the VP and the discussion came to an abrupt end.

The common mistake that most people make is that when they are given feedback about their behaviour, they tend to explain their behaviour by talking about their good intentions and they forget that no matter how good their intentions are, people tend to react to them based on their perceived behaviour and not their intentions. The developmental issue here is that good intentions have to be aligned with the perceived behaviour displayed by the individual to get a balanced response. How does one understand one's perceived behaviour? By the leader constantly seeking feedback from every person they interface with on a day-to-day basis, and by being extremely sensitive to that feedback. A leader should not try to justify behaviour, rather the leader should think seriously of how you as a leader can align that person's perception with your good intentions. In fact, research has found that the gap between a leaders' perception of her behaviour and the perception of others of that behaviour is very small in the case of good leaders.

While Jacques documented his thoughts on several subjects, we did a concurrent survey of the perceptions of the people who interfaced with him on a day-to-day basis. They were given a similar type of questionnaire to answer as the one Jacques was given with the exception that Jacques' questionnaire contained more of an emphasis on his personal values and plans. Appendix B was distributed to the participants of his 360 feedback process.

Appendix B

The following questionnaire is being forwarded to you in preparation for your discussion with Carl Phillips in connection with your confidential feedback on the President of The Garland Group, Jacques Seguin.

The Garland Group is committed to aggressively work toward the development of the world class organization. Several steps have already been taken by the organization in the immediate past to concentrate on this goal. As an integral part of this ongoing effort to build a great company, the leadership has to adopt definite behaviours to spearhead this vision. We all know that for the organization to go from good to great, the leadership has to go from good to great.

Accordingly, Jacques is seeking your considered feedback to help him raise the performance bar, both for him and The Garland Group. Please remember that the purpose of this exercise is to look to future behaviours and actions that Jacques should adopt to act as a role model for the rest of the leadership to help create a great company. It is understood that The Garland Group is a good company. Your responses on how to improve Jacques' behaviour must be made in this context. How should he improve his performance to help move the company from good to great?

It is important to understand at the outset that Jacques cannot do this alone. Therefore, even as you suggest changes in his behaviour, you are making a commitment to give him your total support as he undertakes to change.

Your suggestions in response to this questionnaire will be completely confidential and will only be used as part of a group finding to craft a developmental program for Jacques.

Question 1

Research has shown that great leaders have the following characteristics:

- Very ambitious for their organizations and less so for themselves.

- They make sure that their successors are well set up for the future.

- Humble in a very professional and confident manner.

- Very persistent and diligent.

- Results oriented.

- They give credit to others before giving credit to themselves.

Rate Jacques on each of the above characteristics on a scale of 1 to 5; 1 being low and 5 being high.

On the characteristic that you rate the lowest, what manifested actions would you like to see from Jacques in the next six months to indicate that he is improving in this particular area?

Comment on how you would like Jacques to change his performance for the better in the other characteristics.

Question 2

Does Jacques articulate the common vision of the company clearly, concisely, and effectively? If you feel he does, what are your suggestions for him to do it even better?

Question 3

Further to question 2, critically examine the vision to be a great company in order to answer the following questions:

- Does the vision force the management to make tough choices when the organization is in crisis?

- Inspire the team to align their efforts in a common direction?

- Do employees actually quote the vision when they explain to their friends and relatives what they do in the company?

- Do you think the achievement of the vision will benefit society as a whole?

If your answer is 'yes' to the above questions, give an example to support your answer.

If your answer is 'no' to the above questions, what do you suggest he should do to correct this?

Question 4

Do you think the vision is achievable? If not, what would you suggest should be done to make it more real?

Question 5

Do you feel that the organization has the leadership required to achieve the vision? If not, what do you think should be done to correct this?

Question 6

Do you feel that The Garland Group is correctly organized to achieve the vision with regard to?

- Products and Services

- Markets

- Systems and processes

- Customers

- Suppliers

If the answer to any one of the above questions is 'no', what do you think should be done to correct this?

Question 7

Do you feel that Jacques is a good role model for the expressed values of The Garland Group to become a great company? If not, are there any specific areas in which he can improve his behaviour to better lead the company?

Question 8

Do you trust Jacques implicitly? If you do, what makes you do this? If you question his intentions for whatever reason occasionally, what will help you be more trusting of his intentions?

Question 9

Do you think Jacques always does what he promises to do or does he occasionally forget to follow through? If so, what can he do to improve his performance in this regard?

Question 10

When Jacques sets goals or gives directions for executing a plan of action, do you feel:

- That he has followed an informed, objective, and rigorous thought process before he initiates a course of action?

- That he is realistic in his expectations, in a balanced manner

- That he is amenable to accommodate reasonable changes in the expected results?

- That he permits a fair amount of freedom in the manner in which the goal is achieved?

- That he is meticulous and persistent in the manner in which he follows through to track and encourage the achievement of the expected results?

- Does he take timely and appropriate action to reward good results? By the same token, does he take timely and appropriate corrective action if it is apparent that the expected results will not be achieved?

- Does he inspire accountability and responsibility?

If you think Jacques models the above behaviours, do you feel he needs to raise the bar a bit higher to build The Garland Group into a great company? If he needs to raise the bar, what are your suggested areas?

Question 11

Trust, leadership, customer service, results, innovation, high quality products, strategic planning, business plan execution, management development, team work, communications:

Choose three of the above words or phrases that in your opinion represent Jacques' driving philosophy. Arrange them in the order of priority as you think Jacques sees it. It is understood that Jacques might have more than three of the above items as his driving philosophy, but we need to pick the top three.

Do you think that Jacque's top three priorities are the best priorities for the company?

Question 12

What values do you think The Garland Group should be recognized for in the market? How do you think Jacques should embed these values?

Question 13

Is the Garland Group a transparent organization? If in your opinion it is not, what do you suggest Jacques should do to make it more transparent?

Question 14

Do you believe that the current culture of the organization is conducive to building a great company? If not, name three aspects of the culture that needs to change.

Question 15

In order to help Jacques understand how he is perceived by others, please try to clarify your perceived image of Jacques in the following situations:

- Do you find that Jacques wants to win at all costs and in all situations?

- Do you find Jacques tries to add too much value? Does he add his opinion to any opinion expressed?

- Does Jacques use anger as a management tool?

- Does Jacques withhold information in order to maintain an advantage over others?

- Does Jacques fail to give recognition for fear that he will lose a bargaining stance?

- Does Jacques play favourites?

- Is Jacques a good listener?

- Is Jacques fair in his dealings?

- Does Jacques react positively to negative feedback?

- Do you think Jacques displays good judgment when dealing with day-to-day activity?

- Is Jacques teachable? Does he demonstrate new learning's by his actions?

Are there other aspects of Jacques perceived behaviour that he may not be aware of that needs attention?

Question 16

As we all know, globalization is here to stay. The Garland Group has already taken several steps to deal with this issue. What do you feel needs to change in Jacques leadership style that will model the behaviours required for the leaders of the company to enthusiastically embrace this concept and thus become a great global company?

The above questionnaire is a highly confidential document that is meant specifically for the addressee and should not be discussed with others. Your unbiased opinion is sought to help Jacques understand how he is perceived by others. Thank you for your cooperation.

The leaders of the organization participated in this survey along with select customers and suppliers and they were quite frank and objective in their comments. Carl Phillips personally interviewed each of the participants as opposed to having the participants fill out the questionnaire and not have to explain their comments. The summary of their feedback is given in the next chapter.

Summary of the Chapter

- As a leader you are responsible and accountable for the behaviour of those you lead

- You must walk your talk if you want your impassioned speeches to have effect.

- Dennis Eck, Managing Director and CEO of Coles Meyer, achieved behaviour change in the customer service department by having people observe the reactions of others on the way they treated them.

- People interpret your behaviour as indicative of your intentions.

- You can change the behaviour of others by the way you behave towards them.

- Most leaders believe that if their intentions are honourable when making a change, the change will be perceived as positive.

- The change will be seen as positive if the results are positive; if the results are negative, more often than not, the leader's intentions will be suspect.

- The perceptions of the stakeholders who interfaced with

the leader was sought through a questionnaire and interviews, a copy of the questionnaire is enclosed as Appendix B.

Key Message

A leader's intentions are often misread when the leader's behaviour does not clearly reflect his intentions. Leaders need to walk their talk.

Chapter Nine

Jacques' Reactions To Feedback And Self Improvement

The head of a prestigious ballet school was testing new entrants for training. She watched the new comers being put through their paces for only fifteen minutes and then decided who would be selected for training. When asked how she had made up her mind so fast, she said it was based on a very simple theory that she followed. As she watched the new comers work out, she looked for the ones who tried every stance that the instructor suggested spontaneously, without hesitance, no matter how ridiculous it would make them look. In her experience, these candidates were destined to be champions because of their attitude to self – improvement. The proof lies in the fact that this school has turned out several top class ballet dancers over the years.

Leaders that have risen to top class levels experience something similar when they are undergoing self-development. They are hungry for feedback, but they balk at facing reality. This is a natural tendency. The ones that breakthrough let themselves go spontaneously and deal head on with the facts. Every leader needs to understand this before they start their journey for the top. Jacques' experience brings this point home.

In chapter 8, Carl outlines the gap between leaders' values, beliefs, and intentions versus their team's perceptions which ultimately represent reality. For me, understanding how I was coming across to my team was difficult to gauge. To understand that perception, I had to become comfortable with asking for and receiving feedback from my team. For me, this was a major step in my development. One of the first questions I had to wrestle with was "why?". Given my success to date as a senior executive and leader, why would I open myself up to feedback and make changes? After a time of reflection, I understood that it was my drive for excellence that was propelling me. I faced the reality that if I was not willing to make a change to myself, how could I expect others to make changes? I also realized that, as things evolved, it was a matter of survival for me and that if I did not evolve my capabilities that my effectiveness as a leader would decline over time. So I had to follow the same advice that I was giving to others and jump into the fray. I had to consciously move myself from a state of personal comfort, to personal discomfort. We all know that it's difficult to grow without experiencing discomfort.

In the beginning, when I received feedback that was negative or contrary to my intentions, I became very defensive. I wanted to justify my behaviour and defend my actions. Overcoming that initial reaction is where the "breakthrough" lay for me. As a leader I had to understand that using the feedback to develop new skills, I had to treat this developmental action as an "and" not an "or". I did not need to totally change my approach, but I needed to make modifications and add new skills to achieve better results. What I learned was that by not seeking feedback and by defending my current actions, I was blocking my personal development and the performance of my team. That having been said, it is not an easy blow to take to one's ego, especially if one has been successful in the past based on my use of my existing skills. The challenge lay in me convincing myself that my existing skills were adequate to get me where I was, but they would not get me where I wanted to be in the future. In fact, it was my existing skills that made it possible for me to seek new skills.

Secondly, any changes that were being suggested to my behaviour were not directed at me personally, but rather were being suggested as the behaviour that successful leaders manifested as they led great companies. If I could emulate this behaviour then not only would I be performing as a leader of a great company but better still, I would become a role model for the leaders of my organization and thus generally help raise the quality of leadership for the whole organization.

This is a difficult path to follow and every top class leader will have to face this test. This is the gold standard test of a leader's belief in himself and his personal values. For the leader will have to face a fair amount of hesitance and resistance from the organization. The leaders of my organization had mixed reactions to my actions. There were those who reacted positively and then there were those who were sceptical but were prepared to go along. Then there were those who thought it was a passing phase and if they waited long enough, it would pass. All of these reactions put a great deal of pressure on me to ease off on the changes. More importantly, now more than ever I had to be constant and consistent in my performance. Follow through and follow up became extremely important. Additionally, all this change had to be incorporated into the day-to-day behaviour of the organization as the organization was fighting hard on the operational front.

This necessitated another important communication from me to the leaders. There was an undercurrent of resentment among the people of the organization that the actions being taken to improve the performance of the organization, was an additional exercise that they had to do on top of a heavy operational role that each of them had. It seems unnecessary that one has to explain to the leaders that the changes were not an additional exercise but in fact these changes were what they should be practising in real time to actually improve the effectiveness of their individual roles. This was not a rehearsal but the real thing as they were soon to find out when the economy started going south.

Another important learning for me was the concept of subjective attachment and objective detachment. I was conflicted on how best to lead my team and my team saw this conflict in my leadership style. While I knew that to be a great leader, I had to have a high level of attachment to my team, at the same time, I felt that objective detachment was necessary to make good business decisions. I was trying not to get too emotionally engaged with people in case it clouded my decision making. Since I felt that my primary role as president was to drive the business forward, I chose to not get too personally attached to my team and that this would lead to more objective decision making. Over time I came to understand that to be an effective leader, you need to be attached to your team. My team did not really know who I was and I was concealing the real me. As a result, my team was not fully engaged with me, just as I was not fully engaged with them. As Carl and I worked with the feedback, I concluded that to be an effective leader, I had to get attached to my team while leading and use objective detachment to make good business decisions. I needed to shift gears depending on the circumstance.

In the objective detachment phase of my leadership, I kept personal information to myself, limited social interaction with my team because it was business. Since I was behaving this way, my team did the same with each other and with their teams. As I worked to modify my approach, I increased my social time with my team by setting scheduled individual lunches, golf games, and team dinners and events. I sent less e-mails and made more visits and telephone calls. I set up regular town hall meetings where I took random questions from employees. I established a "Java with Jacques" monthly meeting with a small number of employees. I threw away the scripted speeches and spoke casually and freely at events. I shared more personal information with my team and let "the real me" out at staff meetings. Over time, I saw my relationship with the team change as they started to share more openly with me and with others. I also saw their relationships improve with their peers and with their teams. This elevated the level of teamwork within our company, which started to show in our results.

In an effort to get even more attached to my team, Carl suggested that I complete an exercise which he called "about me". In this exercise, I was to write a one page summary of who I was, what I believed, and what my team could expect from me. I recall having difficulty in completing the write up and having to send Carl numerous drafts. The first draft was a very superficial overview of me. Carl sent it back and said, "Jacques, this is not the real you, do it again." So I took another shot at it, this time revealing slightly more than I had in the prior version. Once again, Carl sent it back. After the third draft and subsequent rejection by Carl, I started to get angry and frustrated with the exercise. I was reluctant to share information with my team that I viewed to be personal. What Carl was doing through his push back was effectively peeling back the layers and gradually easing me into an increased level of comfort and transparency. Once we agreed on the final version, my next task was to sit down with my team and read it to them and then ask them for feedback. The input I received was quite revealing and benefited me as well as my team. For example, in the "about me" write up I described myself as a duck on a pond. While the duck is sitting perfectly still on the water, his feet are moving like crazy under the water. So while I am absorbing the information and thinking through next steps, my team is waiting to see my behaviour. They were viewing this as an inability to make decisions. Because all they could see was a duck sitting still on the pond. At that moment I understood the impact that I was having on my team and they understood that I was simply pondering the decision, versus putting it off or avoiding it all together. This was a major breakthrough in our relationship. I then asked my team to complete the same "about me" exercise and a write up on themselves. From there I established a meeting so we could share these with each other. Out of the nine people invited, four people found convenient "emergencies" to look after to opt out of the meeting. Three people came to the meeting to listen to others but had not prepared a write up. So I cut the meeting short and rescheduled when all could be in attendance and all would have to present their "about me" summary. I led the meeting and started by going first. I felt that by leading the way, the team would get more comfortable. This worked well and over the next three hours, individual team members all shared personal insights and the team got to know each other better.

Every leader should understand that it is important not to waver in the face of opposition. One has to believe firmly in one's actions and follow through. The fact that there is resistance from the team means that they are testing your commitment and belief in your actions. Should you falter, all will be lost. Each member of the team is going through the same doubts and fears that you had. They need you to lead them through this uncertainty. It is not a personal issue against you. They need your confidence in your actions to encourage them on.

In the months following this change and during one of our dealer training sessions, one attendee said that during his many years in our industry and the hundreds of training sessions attended, he had not seen such a tight-knit team of people who enjoy each other's company and give off a family feel. During a subsequent senior leadership team meeting, the EVP of our parent company, who had recently visited our factory for a business review, said that, "Garland has the best team of all of our operating companies."

From there I then asked my team to give me formal and informal feedback and to openly question my behaviour to understand the drivers. In performance review meetings I asked my direct reports for feedback at the end of each session. "What can I do to improve my effectiveness as a leader"? "What can I do to improve your effectiveness in your assignment"? From there I started to get frequent and meaningful feedback. I remember after one of our town hall meetings, one of my direct reports came up to me and said, "Jacques, you did a nice job of emphasizing our success, but you did not recognize enough people." My team was starting to get comfortable and skilled in giving me feedback. They then took this increased confidence and started giving more feedback to their teams so it had a cascading effect. We then modified our annual employee survey to include specific questions around leadership behaviours. Questions such as, "do you trust the leadership team?", "do you receive enough recognition?", "do you feel involved with the decision making process in our business?". These questions were behavioural questions so we could see how our actions were being perceived by the broader team. We took this feedback to heart and worked on modifying our behaviours. Over two years our employee satisfaction scores improved from 70% to 84%.

The process of getting more attached to each other as an executive team was started with the "about me" exercise and is sustained through casual social interaction and behavioural peer feedback. What was initially met with personal and team discomfort and resistance was now accepted and this generated a new way of life at Garland. In the following chapter you will see how my development evolved through the feedback process.

Summary of the Chapter

- Leaders have to be willing to try new things, without hesitance, no matter how it would make them look.

- Leaders have to face the reality that if they are not willing to make a change to themselves, how could they expect others to make changes.

- When getting feedback, overcoming the initial defensive reaction is where the breakthrough lies.

- You do not need to totally change your approach, but you need to make modifications and add new skills to achieve better results.

- To be an effective leader, you need to get attached to your team while leading and use objective detachment to make good business decisions.

- In the "about me" exercise, write a one page summary of who you are, what you believe and what your team can expect from you. Be the first to share it with your team.

- Every leader should understand that it is important not to waver in the face of opposition. One has to believe firmly in one's actions and follow through.

Key Message

Be yourself and use "about me" to accelerate the reveal-ing process.

Chapter Ten

A Summary Of The 360 Degree Feedback On Jacques

The challenge here is that both the leader and the participants in the 360 feedback exercise have to be objective as they face reality. People have to clearly understand the purpose of the exercise. In this case, the purpose was to raise the bar for the performance of the leader in order to help him build a great company. In order to do this, it was emphasized again and again that that there was no hidden agenda or witch hunt involved. The extent to which there was mutual trust and respect for each other in the company is borne out by the fact that people felt comfortable in calling a spade a spade.

Jacques, on the other hand, was open-minded and receptive to the input. He was an ideal subject for development based on the feedback of the people of his organization. This made the exercise much more meaningful and effective. The following is an actual extract from the summary of the findings:

The 360 Degree Feedback Process on Jacques Seguin was well accepted by the participants. They were impressed that Jacques had volunteered to do this exercise. They were also very forth-right and sincere in their input.

It was evident that Jacques is well liked and respected by all the participants.

The participants were very keen to see Jacques succeed in his current role and grow into more responsible roles. More than one participant felt that Jacques was capable of much more and the only thing stopping him from growing was that he was not replaceable in his current role, thus bringing out the fact that he badly needed to find a successor in order for him to grow.

Jacques Seguin as a Person

Jacques is seen as a very intelligent person who, despite the fact that he is outgoing, is really a reserved individual who does not promote himself and is not always given the credit that he is due. He is empathetic, caring, and very genuine. He has very strong convictions and is relentless in his efforts to better his lot. He is very good with people and they believe in him and trust him implicitly. In fact, he is so liked that people are loath to disagree with him or upset him.

He is very insightful and he loves new concepts and innovative thinking. He can go from one concept to another with ease and see the overall connecting links clearly, though he is not at ease trying to explain his understanding in simple language that can be easily implemented. This trait often interferes with his ability to communicate and inspire those who work with him. He comes across as very formal and cut and dried in his statements, which can be somewhat intimidating, especially when he speaks as the boss. He also does not always think it necessary to connect the dots and thus maintain the continuity of a particular course of action. Once he puts something on the table for action, he appears to have moved on and is often left wondering why people are not on the same frequency, or why they need constant reinforcing of the same idea.

He is very socially conscious and takes this for granted. He does not leverage this consciousness to inspire people and motivate them to a higher cause.

He is seen as a very competent and effective sales and marketing person who has spent most of his career in one organization. People seem to feel this is a limiting factor in his decision making. They cannot be farther away from the truth. Jacques is constantly keeping up to date on all fronts that impact on his organization. He needs to work aggressively to change this mistaken image. It is affecting his credibility.

Jacques is a born team player. He is quick to collaborate and give his all for the betterment of the team. On the other hand, he takes this for granted and expects others to have the same principles and motivations. He needs to spend more time building teams, especially in the informal sphere, because this does come to him naturally.

Jacques expects a great deal from people, and this is both a strength and a weakness. Once he delegates a responsibility, he expects the person to take charge and deliver. At that point he appears to be abdicating, and when things do not go as per plan, he often jumps in and gets into the details where he then appears to be micromanaging the individual. He needs to manage more by milestones and hold people accountable for and deal with the consequences expeditiously if they are not met.

Overall Jacques is seen as eminently suited as a leader to lead a great company with some tweaking of his current behaviour.

Action on the 360 Degree Feedback

The broad themes for Jacques' development as enumerated by those who worked with him are:

- Vision: the people needed more clarity and simplicity in the statement, and they needed to feel that it was a commonly held vision that inspired them.

- Succession: Jacques' successor was not in place as also some of the key positions did not have an obvious successor.

- Executive team building: Jacques' executive team did not know Jacques in informal settings. They did not feel comfortable as an executive team.

- Formal versus Informal influencing by Jacques: People felt this was an area for Jacques' development.

- Delegation versus abdication: Jacques needed to delegate and not micro – manage people once he has delegated a job. On the other hand, at times he tends to delegate to the point of abdication.

- Culture: Jacques needed to deal with the different cultures existing in the organization which tends to disrupt team efforts.

- Dealing with superiors: Jacques needed to improve his communication skills when dealing with superiors.

The above developmental needs were to be discussed in detail, and Jacques needed to create a plan of action to develop his new image based on this feedback.

Summary of the Chapter

- This chapter summarizes the findings on Jacques' 360 degree feedback from the stakeholders of the company.

- Both the participants and the subject were refreshingly objective during the process.

- In summary, Jacques was seen as someone who could make it as a leader of a great company. He was also well liked by everyone with whom he interfaced.

- Jacques strengths and developmental aspects are clearly defined and Jacques took the feedback in stride as we shall see from the following chapter.

His developmental needs that emerged were:

- He needed to clarify the vision of the organization and have everyone really buy into it.

- His executives needed to become a better team.

- He needed to improve his influencing skills in an informal setting.

- He needed to concentrate on succession both for his position and for the key positions of the organization.

- He needed to discipline and integrate different cultures in the organization.

- He could be more effective influencing upwards.

Key Message

True leaders seek feedback on their performance constantly to improve their performance. That is why, according to research, there often is very little difference between the self-image of a good leader and the perceptions of that image by others.

Chapter Eleven

Jacques' Personal Development Plan

Based on the 360 feedback, Jacques created a personal development plan. The feedback brought into clear perspective the need for him to:

- Start operating in the real world (Reality).

- Target the common vision and engender commitment (Vision).

- Assemble mutually supportive teams (Team building).

- Reward a disciplined culture (Culture).

- Seed and seek innovative leaders (Succession).

This is the implementation of the Five Star Power process. Jacques launched his personal development by implementing this process. This is not to say that he was not already implementing a similar process in his day to day management of the team. Every good leader adheres to these basic principles, but there is a need to focus on these steps in a more concentrated manner to raise the level of performance of an organization.

Jacques started his personal development plan by dealing with the reality of his leadership and the impact it was having on his team. As we can see from the previous chapter, Jacques was held in great esteem by the leaders and they felt he was doing a good job as CEO. But when pressed to help Jacques become a more effective leader, the team had the following comments to make for his development:

"Jacques needs to push his subordinates to introduce change at a faster pace."

"Jacques needs to be more visibly energetic when reacting to a situation in order to create a sense of urgency and passion in his executive team."

"People cannot keep up with Jacques' concepts and are not sure how they all fit together."

"I sometimes wonder if Jacques is easily distracted once he starts a particular initiative. Too many distractions tend to detract from the intensity and passion of follow up. Maybe he should restrict himself to a manageable number of initiatives."

"Jacques is fairly good at follow up, but sometimes he delegates and then abdicates. As a result things fall through the cracks and I am not sure whether Jacques is trying to avoid facing the bad news or if he forgets."

"He is too tolerant and patient."

"His even keel approach is both positive and negative; he is unflappable but by the same token he could be more passionate."

"He is slow to add his opinion; he needs to speak up and let people know what he is thinking."

"Jacques is very insightful and he expects his audience to get it as fast as he does. He sets himself up to be frustrated when things do not happen as expected. Despite this dynamic, he remains committed to his goals. Because he remains committed to his goals, he expects others to feel the same way. Since others are keen to please him, they do not tell him about the way they feel."

"Jacques needs to personally lead the charge in globalization."

How did Jacques tackle this personal development? Jacques' first step was to face up to reality. There is no doubt that Jacques is a good leader and from his standpoint he was doing his best to be a good leader, but the way he was being perceived by the rest of the team was different to the way he perceived his own behaviour, as can be seen from the sample statements above. It is never easy to deal with the perceptions of others, especially if their perceptions differ from your perceptions of the same behaviour.

In order for a person to change their personal behaviour based on the perceptions of their behaviour by the people they lead, they need to go through three distinct steps:

- They have to be **aware** of the perceptions of others.

- They have to **accept** the perceptions of others as their reality.

- They have to **implement** the change in their behaviour based on the perceptions they want others to have of them.

Jacques' reactions to these three steps were spontaneous and quick. He first embarked on an exercise to get to know his team informally and vice versa. He did this through an exercise that we called "About Me."

This exercise encompassed the following steps:

Jacques would first write up an informal description of how he saw himself, good and bad, and then he circulated that write up among his executive team.

The executive team then got together to discuss Jacques' write up informally. In this informal setting, Jacques would encourage people to discuss how best they can support him, given this write up.

Once Jacques had set the example, he would then suggest that each member of the executive team would do a similar write up and discuss their write up with the rest of the team in a similar manner.

When all the team members had gone through the exercise, Jacques would then initiate the other changes through the executive team, by setting a personal example.

This is by no means an easy exercise, but it is very effective in bonding the executive team together. There were a few executives who hesitated to do the exercise, but if the CEO continues to persist in a persuasive manner, as did Jacques, the team will cooperate. More importantly, the team coalesces and is easier to guide through any further behavioural changes, based on their experiences during this exercise.

Jacques' actual "About Me" write up follows:

About Me

"With me, what you see is what you get. I do not like politics, and individuals who do not say it like it is. At the same time, I believe in being respectful and sensitive to each other's feelings while speaking one's mind.

I believe that people are the key to success and I believe in people – – individuals and teams. While I may not say it or portray it, I care deeply about our people and their well – being. I am intense in my thinking and listening. I am able to see things quickly and "get it". You may perceive this as not listening or caring about what you have to say, but this is usually not the case. I need to slow down and make sure people are clear when I am talking to them. Sometimes I assume that people are following me when they are not. Although I may appear calm and steady on the outside, my mind is always going. I have been compared to a duck sitting still on a pond, yet below the surface, my feet are moving like crazy. I plan and prepare a lot. I sometimes anticipate what we are going to talk about because I have already thought about it ahead of time. I don't tell a lot of jokes but I have a lot of fun. I quietly enjoy things more than I laugh out loud. I tend to see the cup as half full. Sometimes people interpret this as sugar coating the brutal facts. I can't help being optimistic and trying to find the good in things. Most every situation has something good inside it. Please do not misinterpret this – – if the right decision is a tough decision, I will make it.

I might at times appear to be slow to implement a course of action, almost as if I am procrastinating. The reasons I do not act could be one of two cases: either I do not act because I am not totally convinced of the appropriateness of the action, or I am working on the best process to implement the action. If I seem to be taking time to act, you can help me by elaborating on the pros and cons of the course of action or suggest the least disruptive approach to solve the problem. Once I am clear on these points, I am very quick to act.

I am a devoted family man. My family members are the most important people in my life. I still try to play sports and keep up with my teenage boys. I tend to take business a little more seriously because we have a huge responsibility to do the best we can for our people. I need to lighten up but our folks are counting on us so we need to give our best effort. I like to think I am teachable and willing to try new things. I wish my team would feel comfortable enough to challenge me more often so I can learn from them. I think honesty, respect, and integrity are the three most important values. My experiences have shaped these in me.

At work, doing what you said you would do is really important to me. When my team does not do it, it upsets me. I am fanatical about delivering what we promise and tenacious until the end. I think it's important not to let people down. I would prefer never having to follow up with people to see if it got done but I do it because it's an important part of good execution. I expect my team to show initiative, to take charge, and deliver on their accountabilities. I expect people to resolve conflict where they can and escalate when they can't. I do not like unresolved conflict. I take pride in seeing my team develop and achieve their goals and the team's goals.

I would like to spend more time on our vision and strategy with our customers and coaching and developing our team. I really enjoy it and think this is one of my strengths. I think the key to me being able to do this is to have a high performance team in all functions. I am committed to getting this in place. Most every day I get up energized and am thankful that I get to work with wonderful people doing a job that I love. Life is good."

Jacques was complemented by his team several times for initiating such an exercise and for being so forthright in all the discussions. Several team members said that it went a long way in building trust and commitment from all the team players.

The next chapter tells us what Jacques felt and experienced as he went through this stage of the change process.

Summary of the Chapter

- Jacques' development started with the first star which is: Start operating in the real world by asking people for their feedback as to his behaviour. To change his personal behaviour Jacques needs to follow three distinct steps:

- Be aware of the perceptions of others.

- Accept their perceptions as their reality.

- Change his behaviour based on the perceptions that he would want others to have of him.

- Jacques implemented the "About Me" exercise to help himself and his team to know each other.

- Once he had done it, he urged his team to follow suit. It's a good exercise for bringing the team together, which is what it did achieve in the Garland Group.

Key Message

A person's reality regarding your behaviour is based on that person's perceptions of your behaviour. To change that person's reality regarding your behaviour, you have to change that person's perceptions by modifying your behaviour.

Chapter Twelve

Jacques' Personal Development Program

When Carl presented the findings of the 360 feedback exercise, I was favourably impressed by the fact that the team was basically happy with my management style and that they felt that I had the potential to lead a great company. However, when asked to suggest improvements in my operating style, they had some interesting insights to offer. They felt that I was not communicating effectively with them informally. They also felt that the vision of the company was not clear or inspiring. They felt that I needed to build a better team by being more accessible to them. I have to say that this was a little disappointing for me since I believe I was doing all of the above and I was giving my best efforts to the organization. Yet their perceptions were so different from mine.

If they felt this way why had they not told me this before? Was I not listening? Or was I not providing them the right platform for them to be comfortable communicating this to me? I know I needed to improve in order to build a better team, but this was not my perception of my behaviour. It was as though my perceptions were out of sync with that of the team. I had to step back and think clearly of what I was trying to do.

Was this exercise for me to confirm my own perceptions through the team? Or was I interested in understanding the team's perceptions? Did my perceptions count in this instance? My first response to this feedback was filled with questions.

It became clear to me that when I was working with a team and trying to influence them, my perceptions did not matter. The team did things based on their perceptions of my intentions. If their perceptions of my intentions were wrong, then they would not do what I wanted them to do. I needed to understand their perceptions and I needed to communicate my intentions in a more succinct form. I needed to let them know me better and I needed to get closer to them informally.

Even though the above arguments make sense, one still has to deal with one's ego. This is mostly based on how you see yourself. It is true that when evaluating one's self, people tend to see themselves through rose tinted glasses. One very wise CEO summed this up very well. He felt, that "People evaluate themselves based on what they would like to be, and others evaluate those people based on what they are."

I am a fairly pragmatic person. I can take tough feedback and I think that I am very good at learning from any feedback. So after I had made peace with my ego, I began to sift through the feedback and decide on a course of action.

In the meantime, while I was following the process, the executive team was trying to figure out what this process entailed. Was I serious? Was I on a witch hunt? Were they going to be subjected to a similar process? Was this one of my latest fads? Needless to say, the process, like all new things that are introduced into an organization, created an atmosphere of uncertainty. Though the team had a positive attitude and participated sincerely, they did not know what to expect.

For me this process was an excellent tool for self-examination. I knew I had to develop but there was no easy way to do this. There is no doubt that trying to be objective while describing myself to a group of my colleagues as a person and subjecting myself to criticism from them is not easy. This is why I agreed to do the "About Me" exercise.

This exercise had a very good impact all-round. For me it was a milestone of dealing with my personal story with my colleagues and have them open up to me as to their image of me in an informal manner. I learned for instance that my colleagues felt that I was a serious person and my own image of myself was just the opposite. In fact, my family thought that I was hilarious! This told me that I needed to lighten up in the workplace. If I created a serious atmosphere in the workplace, then I would be creating a tenseness that would lead to rigidity and heaviness in the work environment. It also told me that the team did not really know each other. If we did not really know each other, then how could we help each other to grow?

It also brought home the fact that the leaders of teams dictate the behaviour of their teams by the way they personally behave. The moment I decided to loosen up, the executive team started to lighten up and a better camaraderie was established.

The team was hesitant to follow my lead, but they gradually picked up the courage to face the team in a similar manner. I believe that the team was strengthened by this exercise and several mentioned that they found it very beneficial.

Most importantly, the group soon realized that there was no hidden agenda and that we were just trying to grow as a team based on the feedback exercise. This process went a long way in establishing trust and spontaneous interaction between the members of the executive team. Of course, for me this was the starting point for my development because based on this feedback I created a development plan that I started implementing and am still working on it.

What advice do I have for other CEOs and executive leaders? I believe that we need to understand the perception of others because they perform based on how they perceive what you ask of them. Constantly find ways and means of getting feedback on their perceptions. It will tell you where they need your guidance and help.

Secondly, do not underestimate the informal communications network. It is more important than the formal communications network. People need to relate to each other socially in order to work effectively as a team. They get most of this from the informal communications network. Encouraging social interaction is not a waste of work time, it only enhances the effectiveness of the work.

Thirdly, you as an executive are the role model for the rest of the team, so organization effectiveness starts with you!

Summary of the Chapter

- You need to understand your team's perceptions and need to communicate your intentions in a more succinct form.

- If people do not really know each other, then how could

we help each other to grow?

- Constantly find ways and means of getting feedback on your team's perceptions, it will tell you where they need your guidance and help.

- People need to relate to each other socially in order to work effectively as a team.

My Advice to CEOs:

- Your perception of yourself does not really matter when dealing with others; they respond to you based on their perceptions of you. Make it your business to clearly understand their perceptions.

- Do not underestimate the informal organization. It is more important than the formal organization when it comes to dealing with human dynamics.

- You are the role model for the organization and you are watched very closely from what you do to how you do it.

Key Message

The leader must trust and ensure that trust is built within the team. It's the "T" in team.

Chapter Thirteen

The Unwritten Power Of Feedback

Jacques' "About Me" exercise was a raw and deliberate attempt for him and his executive team to face reality. In a way it was a revolutionary process for Garland. Neither CEO nor senior Executive had ever attempted to brazenly open themselves up to critical review in the past. What was Jacques after? Was this a camouflaged witch hunt? Would people be reprimanded in some form down the road for speaking up?

There was considerable hesitance at first, but Jacques set the record straight at the outset. He explained that he needed to understand if his perceptions of himself were the same as their perceptions of him. And if there was a difference, he needed to deal with it. In fact, he was only following up on their comments in the 360 degree exercise that he was aloof and difficult to get to know informally. Even though this was hard for him to accept, it was the reality. He wanted the team to understand that he was the first in the process and that he expected all the executive members to follow up with a similar "About Me" exercise.

The most important step in leadership is having a realistic sense of self. A leader needs to know what this means. More importantly, she needs to understand how others perceive her as a leader because what makes others react to the leaders' wishes has a great deal to do with their perception of her leadership style.

This was the first step in developing a team that could be mutually supportive of each other because they would begin to understand each other's strengths and weaknesses. Jacques was setting an example by starting the ball rolling.

They had commented on the lack of communications at the executive level in the company during the 360 degree feedback session. This process was setting the stage for honest and forthright informal communications at the executive level leading to a new level of trust and commitment as a team.

In Jacques case, the majority of the team members were impressed by Jacques' openness. None of them had ever experienced a situation where the CEO had done such an exercise during their tenure of service, and the average service experience of the members was about fifteen years.

The "About Me" exercise was only the start of Jacques' personal development plan, but it broke the ice. People saw a different side of Jacques that made him more approachable and human. He began to use the informal communication process more extensively.

Jacques began to meet with the executive team socially and even organised games such as tennis with them, creating opportunities for his executives to begin to know the real Jacques and also for him to know each of them. They were creating an informal group whose bonds are stronger than any programmed effort to do so. In fact, during this time we had a group dinner and I was sitting next to one of the senior members of Jacques' team and she said to me, "What have you done to Jacques?" and when I asked what she meant, she replied that he was a different person. He was much more approachable and easier to work with. He seemed to have lightened up considerably.

When people see the real you and say that they like what they see, you know that you are onto a good thing. Jacques had initiated a new culture in the organization. People began to use him as a model and thus embed a new way of dealing with people. He had not really changed as a person but he had taken the feedback that he was given and responded positively to that feedback. What is often not clear to the individual as he is doing it is that he is changing the culture of the organization by merely heeding the feedback.

What message do we have here? People tend to avoid feedback because they fear that the feedback will require them to make drastic changes in their behaviour or more importantly that they will not like the feedback. The fact is that both these deductions are not quite correct. A leader seeks feedback to improve themselves to eventually improve the organization as a whole. If the leader looks at it in this light then everybody wins. This is exactly how Jacques responded to the feedback.

Jacques treated feedback as a perception not as positive or negative, but as the way another person interpreted his behaviour. Jacques decided to change that perception by behaving in a manner that would transmit the message he wanted to convey. Taken in this light, feedback becomes a very positive process in changing the culture of an organization.

Feedback becomes the means by which the organization begins to face reality and deal with it. It is like looking in the mirror and seeing something about yourself that you never saw before; you see an image that makes you see an aspect of yourself that you do not like. What do you do? Do you ignore reality or do you do something about it? You do something about it. Most good leaders seek feedback constantly because they know that feedback is a very useful tool in their developmental process. This is what Jacques launched when he started the "About Me" exercise.

Accordingly the process is repeated throughout the team until each member is well aware of the idiosyncrasies, strengths and developmental areas of each of the other members of the team. Once this is achieved the team then gets together on a regular basis to address any particular members problem in an informal setting. The more this is done, the more trust and mutual support is embedded in the team. This then is the underpinning requirement for a solid executive team.

This exercise is the starting point for individual and team development at the executive team level. The CEO seeks a mentor for his development and the other leaders then commit themselves to do 360 degrees feedback sessions for themselves and their teams. The key here is that there is a constant and consistent follow through in the process at every stage until the whole organization is on the same page and they respect honest and sincere communications and clearly undertake to mutually support each other.

The most important thing to remember while undertaking this process is the follow through. There often is a good amount of enthusiasm as the process is launched, but this begins to drop as the process continues. Here the leader has to make sure that there is no slowing down, no matter what the operational pressures are. If the leader drops the ball, there will be very little return from this process. People have to know that this is going to be standard operating procedure in the organization.

This process also addresses the issue of the right people being on the bus without too many complications. People who are uncomfortable with the process become very obvious. They clearly see a new culture evolving and they are faced with choices, since the pressure to adapt to the new culture is coming at them from all directions. This then is the ultimate confrontation of reality in the workplace.

How does this process help in ensuring that the right people are on the bus?

This process encourages every member to be sincere and honest about their support and developmental needs. They either fit into this environment or they do not. It is highly rewarding for those who fit but those who do not, find it very hard to curb their feelings and therefore come under tremendous scrutiny and pressure from their colleagues to change or move on. Of course those who do neither continue to whine and complain, thus spreading discontent among the easily led. These people must be persuaded to move on.

This form of honesty and no nonsense facing of reality has proven results in the workplace. GE did this all the time in different formats with excellent results. It often seems a bit confrontational at first, but as the process becomes standard operating procedure, it takes root. It is also the start of a team that is hungry for a vision, which is the next step in the development of the leader: to Target the common vision and engender commitment. We are now ready to address the second star of the FIVE STAR POWER process. It might appear that it has taken us a long time to get to the second star, but the fact is that the first star is the foundation stone for all the other stars. Without the first star in place, the other stars do not carry much clout because the leader has nothing to work with.

Summary of the Chapter

- Informal feedback is the purpose of the "About Me" exercise.

- Knowing the strengths and weaknesses in a team is a prerequisite for a team to be mutually supportive.

- Jacques openness as the leader was the catalyst for the team to become more open with each other.

- Acting on feedback helps create a new culture of camaraderie and mutual support in a team.

- Feedback is neither positive nor negative. It is a realistic reflection of how one's behaviour is perceived.

- The most important aspect is the follow through. If the leader drops the ball, the process will be for naught.

- The process also helps to eliminate those who do not subscribe to a winning culture.

Key Message

Feedback is a very powerful tool in the building of a mutually supportive team where joint responsibility and accountability is a given.

Chapter Fourteen

The Second Leadership Star
(s T a r s)
Target the Common Vision and
Engender Commitment

The first star for Jacques, as with any leader, is an ongoing personal developmental activity. We all have to understand that there is no such thing as reaching the zenith of development. Personal development never ends. Jacques continues to work on his personal development as a leader. The second star for a leader deals with the leader's skills for developing the organization. This star requires the leader to target the common vision and engender commitment to it.

Most often a vision statement is confused with a mission statement. I define the difference as someone wisely said, "A vision is what enables you to sleep at night, and a mission helps you to wake you up in the morning." A mission is more tactical and a vision is more strategic. A mission tells you what you need to do and a vision tells you why you do it and the 'why' infuses excitement and passion in what you do. Most importantly, a vision motivates you to be a better person and consequently it helps an organization become an outstanding organization.

Every person has an intrinsic need to follow a goal that would help the person self-actualize their capabilities and interests. The common problem is that they often cannot articulate that intrinsic need. We call it a personal vision.

Every person has a personal vision. Despite having this vision, not every person is able to articulate this intrinsic need. They need help. However, if you do not help them by defining this unstated vision, they become mere workers doing what they are told to do, not less or more. In every organization there is an unstated vision in each person that a leader needs to tap and enunciate. There often is a common thread in each of these visions, because there are universal needs that turn on people generally, especially if the people are all part of a team working together to achieve a common goal. Once the leader is able to define the common vision, the organization begins to resonate and people do what the organization needs done in order to achieve the common vision. People fall in line enthusiastically. There is a palpable sense of purpose and commitment. Everyone is engaged and the results will speak for themselves.

Why do people have difficulty articulating their personal visions? It is because they lack confidence in their ability to achieve their visions. A vision is a big statement that individuals make about themselves, and having made it, reality strikes. Since they have not been there before, their resolve falters.

Do we feel that we cannot manage such a broad concept incorporating our ability to deal effectively with work, family, and all our relationships with the community and the world at large? The word 'vision' is all encompassing and most of us do not believe that we can actually say we have a vision with conviction.

Yet deep within us there is an intrinsic need to address all these issues in life and to feel that we have done the best we could for each of them. A leader is able to articulate this common thread in the organization as a group vision that is shared by the whole team in such a manner that individuals begin to believe that they can actually achieve this vision as a team. Once they believe, they become zealous and committed.

Making an unstated vision tangible is like the development of the personal computer by Steve Jobs and Steve Wozniak in the launching of Apple Computers. By developing the personal computer, they actually defined the needs of thousands of people who wanted a device like this but did not know how to articulate their needs and translate those needs into a tangible product. Once Jobs and Wozniak articulated the common vision in physical terms, they eventually could not keep up with the demand for the personal computer. Everyone wanted one. But before people actually saw the PC physically, they could not articulate what they wanted. In other words, good leaders have the ability to so articulate the common vision (which remains mostly in the subconscious of most members of an organization) that they are able to make the subconscious needs of the team tangible and meaningful. The work of a leader becomes very simple once this happens. Have you ever tried to sway believers from their beliefs? A true believer is pretty unshakable. So also are true believers in a vision.

So what then are the key sets of principles and guiding practices that are needed for a personal vision to become a shared vision and accordingly help galvanize an organization into superior performance?

On numerous occasions I have asked people in an organization to articulate their vision statement. I did this again in the case of an off-site meeting with Garland. The results are almost always the same – – they all have to take out the written version of their vision statements and read it out. Why did they have to do this? They could not recall the statement from memory. Right there lies the first hurdle. If you cannot recall the vision without referring to a written page, then you will not use it as an inspiration to guide you. Unless, of course, you read it every time you do something at work. So the first principle to follow is to define the vision in a simple, short set of words that will be easy to remember. For instance Ford had "Public transportation for the masses." Or Polaroid had "Instant Photography."

How does one get these words? I guess everyone has heard the sentence of a letter that a person was writing to a friend in a bit of a hurry--"I am sorry that I cannot write you a shorter letter since I am in a bit of a hurry." Expressing one's self in succinct, clearly understandable terms requires much thought and time. So every vision statement must be developed with the input from every member of the organization in simple understandable terms. Because everyone in the organization must be able to clearly understand the vision statement and commit to it, not just to memorize it and repeat it without actually understanding or believing in it. Most vision statements are expressed in such lofty terms that very few really understand it or use it effectively.

In Garland there was initial resistance to restating the vision statement in these simple terms, but Jacques persisted and went through several iterations before the vision statement caught on and the test of it was when a senior manager actually started his talk to customers by quoting the vision statement as the company's reason for being.

How then does one engender commitment to the vision? The most important step is getting everyone to participate in articulating it. While doing this one must ensure that:

- The vision truly reflects what the organization wants to achieve.

- The vision statement is short and simply stated.

- The vision statement embodies an inspirational message.

- Everyone in the organization must be able to use it in their job daily.

The second most important step is that every executive re-enforces the vision statement on a day-to-day basis with everyone that they deal with, for example the organization, customers, suppliers, investors, and the community at large. By the executives setting the example, the rest of the organization will follow suit.

The third most important step is that the casting of the yearly operational plan must incorporate the vision statement. In other words, the plan works backwards from the vision statement. Individual and group targets are tied to the achievement of the vision as are the rewards, promotions, and recognition awards.

Concurrent to these activities, the next most important step that the leader has to address is the next star which is "Assembling mutually supporting teams" within the organization. The details of which will be addressed next, but in the next chapter Jacques will tell us what happened in the organization as he initiated actions to restate the vision.

Summary of the Chapter

- Personal development never ends. This is the purpose of the first star-adjusting your behaviour to the real world.

- The next star is the T in the word STARS—Target the common vision and engender commitment.

- A mission tells you what to do and a vision tells you why you need to do it. The why infuses you with passion and excitement in what you do.

- Every person has a personal vision whether stated or not.

- The leader needs to identify the common thread in the personal visions of the people in the organization and adopt the common vision.

- Vision statements should be simple; a short set of words that will be easily remembered so that everyone in the organization can use it in their jobs daily.

The three important steps for embedding the vision in an organization are:

- Everyone should participate in articulating the vision statement.

- Every leader should re-enforce the vision statement at every opportunity with all stakeholders.

- The yearly operational plan of an organization should be so shaped around the vision statement, that every milestone of the plan re-enforces the vision.

Key Message

For a group of people to passionately implement a vision, they each need to see their own personal vision embedded in the shared vision statement.

Chapter Fifteen

Creating a Common Vision Statement

I have always believed in the power of personal visions. People have fought and laid down their lives because they believed in a cause or had a vision. We are all familiar with Martin Luther King's statement, "I have a dream" and how powerfully it resonated throughout a country. I also believe that most people want to make a positive contribution in their lives and connecting their individual contribution to an inspiring team or company vision is a real motivator.

I have tried to leverage people's efforts by persuading them and using logic and common sense to focus their efforts so that they could achieve the company goals for their own good and for the good of the company. Knowing that this was not enough, our team developed a vision that was well articulated, though somewhat lengthy. We tried to be all inclusive in our vision statements and therefore we tended to make the statement somewhat wordy. Our first vision statement was ,"We will exceed the expectations of our global customers and shareholders by providing superior quality, innovative food-service equipment solutions. Our exceptional people listen and we deliver what we promise." So while it defined what we were trying to do and how we would create value, it did not inspire the team. This is a common failing of most companies. If a vision statement is too long and complicated, it will not be effectively used as a guide to implement a business plan.

We also had a mission statement that succinctly articulated the three pronged tactics that we would follow to achieve our vision. The company was committed to this mission statement. We implemented these tactics meticulously to the best of our abilities. We did a good job of following instructions to the letter, doing our best to fulfill our responsibilities, because we liked our jobs and the security that came with it. But were we charged up with passion for a greater cause? Were we motivated to the point that failure was not an option? The answer was no. We all know that leaders have to own and believe in a greater cause to go the extra mile when given a responsibility.

When Carl conducted in-depth interviews with my senior leaders, he got some feedback which made him feel that they were not excited by the vision statement of the company. It was also evident that the concept of a vision was not clearly understood and therefore not really necessary to inspire people when faced with failure. They felt that they were doing just fine with what they had. I was quite surprised, however, when Carl asked the leaders as a group to repeat the vision statement of the company, that not one of the leaders could do it. They had to refer to the pamphlet and read it out. I have to admit that I had to consistently rehearse it and made frequent mistakes when reciting it. I knew that if the leaders could not repeat it, there was no chance that the rest of the team could. Most vision statements are motherhood statements that are so general in nature that they are mere words of good intentions and therefore not easily recalled or used in the day-to-day driving of the business. So why have a vision statement? It is nice to have and generally seen as a necessity, but apart from completing what seems like an accepted drill, it is not used for any specific purpose. In fact, it is not surprising how similar most vision statements are and it would not be out of place to use most of the same words of the vision for any company because they are only general statements of good intentions.

My understanding of a vision statement is that it should be so simply stated that every individual in the company can not only understand it but also so relate to it that they enjoy using it in their day to day activities of running the business (see chapter fourteen). It becomes a rallying call around which every member of the organization is proud to unite. It becomes embedded in their every day vocabulary and they find it hard to describe what they do without using the words of the vision statement. The vision statement expresses in very succinct terms the raison d'être of the organization. Though the leaders in Garland were not too clear about the vision of the organization, Carl found that leaders in the organization could clearly remember the mission statement because it drove their day-to-day tactical activity. They used the statements to function effectively in their jobs and they took pride in the fact that they were doing a good job against the parameters of the job. They were not stretching themselves to function at a higher level nor were they passionately inspired to reach out for a greater cause other than making and selling a product or a service. To me that was limiting and restrictive from an innovative growth standpoint, and I felt that we were leaving a lot of opportunities on the table. We needed to engage all of our employees at the emotional level and tap into their innovative skills and passion for growth to become a great organization.

This also told me that I was leading a group of tactically focused leaders who needed to rise above being only tactically effective. By doing this they were leaving most of the burden of strategic thinking to me as the CEO. In so doing, they forced me to constantly force the implementation of the strategic plan. Not only is this a heavy burden to carry for a CEO, but it is very limiting for the company. The total brain power of the leaders of the organization was not being effectively used from a strategic standpoint. They needed a rallying call to unite them. The vision statement needed to be revisited. If the leaders had to refer to the written vision statement then they were not using that statement for their day-to-day guidance at work. It was in their minds and not in their hearts. They lacked a passionate commitment to a cause, though they felt the need to be good corporate citizens and do their best to achieve the mission. I needed their joint commitment and passion behind a vision that would put fire in the bellies of the whole organization and thereby embed a visionary perspective in everything that they did. They needed to believe in a greater cause that would stimulate them to exceed their own expectations.

The challenge that I faced was to be able convey this message to the leaders so that they would see the need for a more meaningful vision statement. This was not an easy task.

I started off by suggesting that each of the leaders in my executive committee should attempt to articulate such a vision statement so that the person on the floor would relate to it and use it in their daily work activity. It was very interesting to see that the team initially resisted my approach and said that our current statement was "good enough". I insisted that we follow through with the exercise. The executive committee each attempted to articulate their versions of the vision statement, then we met and discussed the statements.

Having done this exercise, we then created a competition for the leaders at the next level of the organization to produce the best vision statement for a cash prize. Not surprisingly this level of leaders came up with some very exciting vision statements. We then took the winning statement into a special executive committee meeting and incorporated most of the words of the winning vision statement into the final version and communicated this to the rest of the organization. The statement was extremely well received and immediately adopted.

The final vision statement was: "We bring innovation into the world's kitchens."

Once the vision statement was communicated throughout the organization, it then became the job of every leader at every level of the organization to constantly refer to it with the people in the organization, with customers, suppliers, and all stakeholders. Most importantly, they were encouraged to use the statement as a yardstick of measure whenever they were implementing the operational plan of the company to feel the vision statement in action. The vision statement was embedded into the business plan of the organization and the excitement that the statement generated at every level was clearly visible in the way things were done in the organization.

My greatest pleasure after these actions were implemented was to be told after we won a major global contract that the customer was reassured of our ability to meet their standards by the solid commitment of the leaders to an inspiring vision statement.

The vision statement was the beginning of a new era in the organization. The leaders began to realize that they had to adopt a strategic perspective in everything that they did in their day-to-day activities in order to implement the vision. This was not easy for them to do because they were used to looking at me for guidance when faced with a strategic challenge. I had created that behaviour through my own behaviour. It was also a new challenge for me. I had to learn to look back at them and tell them to use their initiative as they implemented the vision statement in action, instead of responding as I did in the past with a solution. I recall that during one of our vision meetings, one of the executives came up to me and said, "this is crazy, why don't you just tell us what to do so we can just get on with it?" I resisted his approach and persevered with the process. I had to show them that I trusted them and depended on them to come through in a crunch. This process that I followed had to be duplicated again by my direct reports to the people under them and so on down the line until it reached every person on the factory floor.

It is important to emphasize the fact that one has to constantly repeat and follow through on the process as often as it is necessary for the concept to really be consistently reflected in the behaviour of every individual of the organization. I am still working on this even as I write this, more than four years later. It's a marathon, not a sprint, but our business performance has dramatically improved as a result.

Summary of the Chapter

- People want to make a positive contribution in their lives and connecting their individual contribution to an inspiring team or company vision is a real motivator.

- When logic prevails and a vision statement becomes too long and complicated, it will not be effectively used as a guide to implement a business plan.

- Leaders have to own and believe in a greater cause to go the extra mile.

- Most vision statements are motherhood statements that are so general in nature that they are mere words of good intentions and therefore not easily recalled or used in the day-to-day driving of the business.

- Leaders need to engage all of the employees at the emotional level and tap into their innovative skills and passions to become a great organization.

- It is the job of every leader, at every level of the organization, to constantly refer to the vision statement with the people in the organization, customers, suppliers, and all stakeholders.

- The vision statement must become the yardstick by which we measure everything that we do in the organization, specifically by embedding it in the operational plan.

Key Message

Vision statements should be spoken, not read from bulletin boards. They should make every team member feel proud and inspired to do the work because they want to excel. This is every individual's most cherished desire.

Chapter Sixteen

The Third Leadership Star
(s t A r s)
Assembling Mutually Supportive Teams

One of the most overused words in any leadership book is the word "Team". Even though the word is always used with very good intentions, it is seldom if ever comprehended in its entirety. The word "team" conjures up several meanings but the core issue that makes a team work is often not emphasized. The core issue is: The leader of a team provides the nucleus model behaviour that embodies mature emotional commitment to a vision, trust and respect in a team. Concentrate on the right type of leader and you will nurture the right type of team.

For an individual to be an effective member of a team, a high level of mature emotional commitment to a mutually shared goal of a group is required. The main ingredients of this commitment are an individual's emotional maturity coupled with the ability of an individual to put the interests of the group ahead of the individual's interests. All of the foregoing demands an exceptional bond of mutual trust among all members of a group to qualify as a team; and trust cannot exist without mutual respect between members of a team. All of these issues are underpinned by the consistency of the leaders' behaviour versus their verbal commitments.

In order for a group to be truly committed to a cause, there are several prerequisites that have to be present:

- An inspiring leader.

- A worthy cause (a believable mission).

- A committed group of people to that cause.

- Mutual respect between the members of the group.

- A mutually agreed upon value system in the group.

- A mutually agreed upon work approach in the group.

- A mutually agreed upon reward system.

So far in this book we have dealt with the first three bullets in this list. In this chapter we will deal with the next three bullets. Respect for an individual is earned by the fact that the individual has a strong value system and lives by those values on a day-to-day basis.

Most often than not, leaders underestimate the importance of living their stated values on a daily basis. When there is a difference between the values that we say and believe that we use and those that we actually use, there is a serious repercussion for the leader and for those around the leader. The difference between these two perspectives is critical to the level of respect that an individual gets: the bigger the difference, the less respect we have for that individual. When we have a group of leaders who are respected for their values and the fact that they live by them, we then have the makings of a team. Remember, you can only lead people where you are prepared to venture forth yourself.

The main issue to understand about building a team is that the leader of the team understands the importance of modelling the behaviour that they expect of the team. You can have what seems to be key to making a team work, for example a meaningful vision and a committed group of people, but if you have a leader who does not provide a live example for the team then the team will not perform effectively. They will not respect nor trust the leader and accordingly not respect nor trust their team members.

It is not uncommon for the leaders of teams to lay down the expected behaviour for the team and be quite oblivious of the fact that the rules apply to the leader also. In fact, if the leader does not model the expected new behaviour there will be little or no attention paid by the team to the new behaviour.

With this in mind, Jacques concentrated his efforts on creating a team at the executive leadership level by modelling the new behaviour himself first. He opened himself up to the team by describing his strengths and weaknesses. He then sought their feedback as to their perceptions of his behaviour and what they would like him to change. He then started acting on the feedback and sought their feedback six months after to gauge the effect his changed behaviour had on the leaders.

At the same time, Jacques had the leaders in his executive committee do the same exercise with their colleagues. He also instructed them to cascade the process downwards to the next level and onwards until it reached the person on the manufacturing floor.

This process requires several iterations until the organization adopts a strong team focus and once this is achieved it becomes easy to get the team to passionately follow through on all the points enumerated above as prerequisites for an effective team.

This process of course is not as easy as it sounds. There is a continuous need for coaching and motivating of leaders at all levels as each leader also strives to model the expected behaviour themselves. But the results are extremely satisfying and each little success motivates the teams to reach higher levels of performance.

A leader needs to concentrate on building leaders. How does a leader do this? The leader needs to focus all efforts on her personal behaviour and the behaviour of her direct reports. The focus on the direct reports involves a concentrated effort on making the direct reports better leaders. This concentration includes intensive coaching, mentoring, and motivating them to reach still higher levels of performance. All of these activities are done both during formal and informal meetings to consistently bond and understand where each team member is coming from. Concurrent to this concentrated effort on the direct reports, the direct reports are also encouraged to focus their efforts on their direct reports. The process ensures that the same message travels through the leaders at all levels down to the shop floor.

When a process like this is meticulously followed, a real team begins to coalesce. Leaders learn that their role is to create more leaders. By creating leaders they are ensuring that each person in the organization begins to take a pride in themselves and behave as leaders should. They begin to truly understand the meaning of mutual respect, trust, and mature emotional commitment. As these qualities are emphasized the organization starts to function as a well-oiled machine or a true team.

A great team that truly understands and intimately relates to the critical issues that help nurture a force that is to be reckoned with requires a team leader who personally embodies these characteristics. In fact, most of the reasons why an organization does not function at its optimum performance level can be attributed to the lack of effective teams and in turn this means the absence of true and effective leadership of those teams.

Jacques will tell you in the next chapter about the challenges that he faced while applying these concepts to his team.

Summary of the Chapter

- Concentrate on the right type of leader and you will nurture the right type of team.

- The main ingredients of a team are mature emotional commitment to a mutually shared goal where every member puts the interests of the group ahead of their own interests.

True commitment to a goal requires:

- An inspiring leader

- A worthy cause

- A committed group of people

- Mutual respect between members

- A common value system

- A common work approach

- A common reward system

- If you have all of the above in a team but the leader does not model the code of behaviour consistently, the team will collapse.

- Leaders need to coach and mentor their teams constantly. It takes several iterations to embed the essentials of a team.

- If you want to embed mutual accountability and responsibility in a team, follow the Five Star process meticulously.

Key Message

A team's motto should be, "One for all and all for one." Every member should subscribe to this concept and implement it religiously.

Chapter Seventeen

Developing Mutually Supportive Teams
– Its Hard Work
(s t A r s)

Assembling a great team is one of the most difficult challenges that a leader faces. As I grew within our company, my early view of team building was to assemble a team of technically competent people and let strategy, tactics and the passing of time develop the teamwork. I complemented this with the typical off-site meetings but found that the burst of enthusiasm was short lived and people defaulted to individual play. Working with Carl, I learned that the foundational building block for a team was me. Firstly, I had to put my ego and personal ambition aside and put the team's success first. This was a major shift for me requiring both a change in my thinking and my behaviours. I came to realize that my success as a CEO was an outcome of the team's success and therefore, building a team of people who were not only technically competent but were also committed to each other and to the team's goals was the key to my success. Carl reinforced the need for me to:

- Ensure mutual respect between the members of the group.

- Develop a mutually agreed upon value system in the group.

- Define a mutually agreed upon work approach in the group.

- Ensure a mutually agreed upon reward system.

As leaders we all know aligned values are a key to building strong teams. For me, these values are honesty, integrity, and respect. While these were very clear to me, why was my team's behaviours not consistently aligned to these values? In the end it came down to two things:

1. I had not clearly articulated these values. My direct reports had to interpret what our values were and, left to their own interpretations, were not always or directly aligned. This caused much friction amongst the team and frustrations. In the end, I had to define and communicate these values which set a standard for current and new employees of our company. These values were posted everywhere in our company. This standard was tested many times and I recall agonizing over decisions to take action on employees who were getting good results but their behaviours were not in line with the standard. In the end, these employees left our company and looking back now the team was stronger for it and our results improved.

2. Exposing my true self so people could see me modelling the values. In earlier chapters of the book I shared my experience with the "about me" exercise. This exercise is a critical part of the team building process. While it's a good idea to define values, it's just as important to model them AND to have people see you modelling them.

By being yourself in everyday situations, people see your consistent commitment to the values which, builds trust and respect.

Beliefs are built through a series of consistent behaviours, experienced over and over again. You can't just ask people to trust you, you have to earn it over time.

As I exposed my true self, trust started to build and we became more comfortable as a team. My team felt more confident and they started to let their true self be exposed. Teamwork reached a new level and we had more open and candid discussions about our team's performance and we made better decisions. Mutual accountability increased with team members challenging each other openly but positively. Since they now trusted me and each other, they felt safe in taking on more difficult topics. Speed and efficiency improved as the team was more focused on the team's performance than the politics of who wins and who loses. Team members frequently volunteered to cover each other during times of tough deadlines and resource crunches. Attendance at team dinners, which were held once per month, increased as team members enjoyed spending time together.

As our team and business performance improved, I was eager to see this passed on to the next level in our company. While I felt that much of it would just cascade down naturally, I asked each of my direct reports to schedule an "about me" session with their teams to start the process. While I was pleased with the progress made within my team, taking the process down to the next level was more difficult. Initially, one of my direct reports followed through and the six others found convenient excuses to push it off. Recognizing that this was not going to happen without some effort, I started to tighten the schedule and ask for commitments from the team. Two other members of the team responded. Of those four final leaders that resisted, two had to be reassigned to roles where they could contribute as individuals, and the two others left the company. Replacements were put in place that fit well within my team of direct reports and were able to execute and build strong teams. A key lesson learned for me was that while some leaders have the values to be part of a mutually supportive team and make excellent team members, they lack the capability to lead and build mutually supportive teams.

With the executive team in place, we wrote a team charter (see appendix A) that defined who we are and how we are expected to behave. We reviewed it together and committed to it as a team. We developed a process map for our company that defined how we did work within our company. We educated all of our employees on this process map. This resulted in improved teamwork and efficiency. We also changed the bonus system so all employees were rewarded on the team's performance. This was a change from the functional reward system that we had in place. We also instituted an informal thank you recognition system where the executive team would catch people doing things right and publicly praise employees.

My focus then shifted to maintaining the team chemistry, guarding against misaligned behaviours and promoting the company values with each new hire. I also shifted to building my direct reports up as leaders. I took a personal interest in each of my direct reports personal goals and worked with them on development plans. I set regular meetings to track their progress and coach them along their journey. We celebrated their success together and I motivated them when they needed it. Once again, I had more success with some than others but on the whole, I could see progress.

I set a firm expectation that all my direct reports spend time to develop new leaders within their teams and as a result, we saw more jobs and promotions filled from internal talent. As an outcome, when associates see others getting promoted, it inspires them and increases their commitment to the company, thus improving the overall performance of the team.

In the end, the formula for building mutually supportive teams is clear:

1. Develop a clear common goal, set a standard on values, be yourself, and model the values to build trust and respect.

2. Coach and build your team members capabilities so they can build their teams. Define and communicate how the company approaches work, align the reward system to promote teamwork.

3. Sustain the gains and where needed, stand firm and make adjustments on people and behaviours that are undermining the team's performance.

Summary of Chapter

- Assembling a great team is one of the most difficult challenges that a leader faces.

- The leader has to put her ego and personal ambition aside and put the team's success first.

- The values must be clearly articulated. If not, people are left to interpret the values and left to their own interpretations, they will not always be directly aligned.

- The standard will be tested many times and the leader needs to take action to protect and nurture the values.

- Engage your team in developing a team charter (see appendix A) that defines the role and goal of the team and how it is expected to behave.

- Develop a process map for your company that defines how the work will be done in your company.

- Set a firm expectation that all your direct reports spend time to develop new leaders within their teams.

Key Message

Be ready to work hard, reinforce good team behaviors, and make tough decisions on people that cannot work in or build a team. Teamwork trumps everything else.

Appendix A

The Garland Group Executive Committee - Building a great company through individual and team excellence!

STRATEGY- CAPABILITY- COMMITTMENT

The Executive Committee is responsible for defining the vision of the company, owning it, and communicating it so effectively that the whole organization is mobilized, committed and driven to achieve it. As importantly, the Executive Committee needs to develop a great organization...an organization of which each stakeholder can be proud of!

We develop, continually monitor and evolve our strategy and ensure that we have appropriate capability to achieve it. Executive Committee members are required to take initiative to stay current on global economic and industry trends, company performance and global best practices. We ensure that every member of the Executive Committee is mutually accountable and responsible for meaningful and innovative contributions towards the effective performance of the Executive Committee.

We, the Executive Committee, believe that a "high performance executive committee" is the cornerstone of building a "high performance team" capable of achieving our Vision and our short term goals. We are committed to making this happen and we achieve this by being examples of our stated values and behaviors.

The Executive Committee is guided by the following guidelines:

1) Through our personal behaviors, we will build the company culture around our stated values and behaviors. While we model them, we also nurture and defend them in our everyday interactions.

2) We will always respect, but challenge each other and our thinking. Healthy conflict is encouraged but when it arises, we seek to resolve it quickly. Unresolved conflict is a killer of speed, innovation, teamwork and achievement of results. Preferably, this can be done with "one on one" interaction. If the resolution cannot be achieved due to resource conflicts, both parties will escalate the decision making to the appropriate person. Once a decision is made, we will accept it and implement it with our full support and commitment.

3) We will act as models for personal improvement...being the first to participate... getting/staying actively involved... generating enthusiasm amongst others by demonstrating our teach ability.

4) We will support each other and the achievement of our common goals. Whenever possible, we will collaborate to assist each other in achieving our goals.

5) We will view the "making" of new leaders as a core activity and we will take personal interest and be actively involved with teaching and developing our people.

As the Chair of the Executive Committee, I am committed to making a "high performance Executive Committee" a reality and the ultimate example of teamwork within Enodis and the Global Foodservice Industry.

Enodis

Chapter Eighteen

The Fourth Leadership Star
(s t a R s)
Reward a Disciplined Culture

There is an old management cliché that says, "What gets rewarded gets done." The word 'rewards' in the workplace is often associated solely with such things as money, stock, perks, prestige, position, and promotion. There is another perspective on rewards which is very powerful for an employee, and that is personal pride and self-worth. This aspect deals with the persons being proud of their achievements and their competence and their contribution to society as a whole. When an individual is recognized and rewarded for these efforts, the reward touches a special button of the individual's emotional need to excel and be totally committed to the work. The individual exudes a passion for the type of work being done because it contributes to self-fulfillment and personal enjoyment. The other external rewards such as money are good to have and play a part in preventing the person from being de-motivated.

How does a leader create an environment that rewards a disciplined culture? A leader has to first and foremost model a disciplined culture. This means that the leader must have a passion for the organization's vision and therefore be prepared to measure every personal action with the key tenets of the vision. Only then will the leader earn the respect of the organization and have the clout to enforce a disciplined culture in the organization.

Jacques laid down the team charter (See Appendix A of chapter 17) for his executive committee, which clearly defined their behaviour to create a disciplined culture in Garland. This charter concentrates on the intrinsic rewards of the leaders and how they can model this behaviour for the rest of the organization. The buck stops here. Or does it? I prefer to say that the buck starts here.

The key part of the charter is where the CEO makes a written commitment, "As the chair of the Executive Committee, I am committed to making a high performing executive committee a reality and the ultimate example of teamwork."

This placed a very high responsibility on Jacques personally to perform and be accountable to any and every member of the organization for his behaviour, as it also did apply to the executive committee.

As a leader therefore the buck really does not stop here, it actually starts here. This is not as easy as it seems. You make a commitment and write the commitment down and the others will follow right? Wrong. The words mean nothing until they are reflected in your behaviour. Here starts the hard part. It is not what you tell people to do, it is what you do that dictates what the others in your organization will do. You want to lead a great organization? Then you have to strive to be a great leader. You have to live the vision.

The vision statement for Garland is "We bring innovation into the world's kitchens" and in order to live this vision, you need to be disciplined. How does this work exactly? The way it works is that the leaders have a strict code of conduct that they nurture in all the people that they lead. The people look to the leaders to be living examples for them. In fact, when the leaders do what they profess that they believe in, the people do not have to be rewarded for their behaviour; they consider their disciplined behaviour as normal. When this happens, you have established a disciplined culture. When anyone does not behave in the expected manner, the group automatically reacts negatively towards the individual to bring the person back on track.

The tough part is to pattern all your behaviour to further the vision. In other words every time you go to initiate behaviour as a leader, you ask yourself, "How does this help bring innovation to the world's kitchens?" If the other stars of the FIVE STAR POWER process that we have already enunciated in earlier chapters are in place, for example leaders understand and deal effectively with reality, they have developed and communicated a common vision, and they have assembled a great team, it will not be difficult for them to create a disciplined culture in the organization. They have already sowed the seeds of a disciplined culture by doing the above. That is why it is important to implement this process sequentially.

Embedding a culture in an organization takes time. Therefore, it is imperative for the leaders of the organization to be consistent and predictable in their day to day behaviour over the long haul. The leaders are the key to this particular exercise. The slightest wavering on their part by even one leader can disrupt the process and taint the culture.

In this light, the CEO has a big responsibility. If the CEO permits a leader to deviate, other leaders will follow suit with their direct reports and so the contamination of the culture goes right through the organization. It is often worthwhile for that leader to be removed if they do not respond to coaching. On the other hand, committed leaders are worth their weight in gold. They will generate tremendous excitement and commitment to the implementation of the vision.

In order to establish a disciplined culture one needs to establish a written code of behaviour that spells out how the organization conducts business. As long as a person follows the code of conduct, leaders should reward and positively reinforce their behaviour and permit them as much freedom and independence as they can handle. People thrive when they feel free to use their initiative and innovative skills to make things happen.

Most often people view the concept of a disciplined culture as being controlling. This is not true. A disciplined cultured team is one that respects and obeys a higher code of behaviour because the behaviour makes them better people and the organization as a whole benefits from it. The people willingly subscribe to that behaviour because they want to be better people.

Which brings up another important aspect on the development of a code of behaviour: when a leader writes out a code of behaviour and then mandates that everyone should toe the line, we have a control situation. The culture will develop cracks under pressure. If, on the other hand, the leader involves everyone in the development of the code, and also gets them to commit to religiously follow the code, then we have the foundation for a disciplined culture that is willingly followed and enforced by the people themselves.

What would motivate employees to voluntarily seek a higher code of conduct? They have to think of the business as owners. They have to be engaged in the business and relate to the overall goals of a business.

This gap in the two perspectives does not help an organization establish a disciplined culture. In order to develop self-disciplined people in an organization, we need to have every person thinking as an owner. We need to create a transparent environment. Transparency engenders trust; trust engenders commitment; commitment creates owners; owners seek the best for an organization, and this generates a disciplined culture. By these actions the above two perspectives merge and pull together.

So what is the start of this process? It is that the leaders help develop a written code of conduct that reflects the group's common thinking for the business. The leaders have to use this code as a guide for their behaviour and be prepared to be held accountable for their actions. When this happens, the rest of the organization follows.

In the following chapter Jacques will tells us how he managed to implement his team charter wherein Garland had defined their code of conduct for their business and thus helped move the organization towards a disciplined cultured company.

Summary of the Chapter

- 'What gets rewarded gets done' and the best reward you can give to individuals to be an effective part of a team is to promote self-respect, self-pride, and self-actualization amongst every member of the team.

- A leader has to first earn the respect of a team to develop a disciplined culture in the team.

- A values statement should be supported by a commitment to implement the vales on a day to day basis by every member of the team.

- To lead a disciplined organization, you have to be a disciplined person consistently as a leader.

- A disciplined culture is not a controlling culture for control stifles an organization. People are disciplined because they want to be better people and to belong to a better organization.

- Everyone participates in defining a code of behaviour. It therefore becomes easy to enforce it. This is the beginning of everyone thinking and behaving as owners.

Key Message

A disciplined culture is established when people are self-disciplined and are guided in their behaviour by participating in developing a code of behaviour and following that code meticulously.

Chapter Nineteen

Establishing a Disciplined Culture
(S t a R s)

Creating, rewarding, and sustaining a disciplined culture is key to a company's success. How many companies do we know where culture and employee behaviors are erratic? Yet when we meet various employees from other companies, they all seem to fit and feel the same to us? Most people have good intentions and once they understand the expectations for disciplined behaviors, they will work to align themselves to it. Having said this, the journey is a challenging one as with other elements of change, it requires that people learn and embrace new behaviors to replace the existing ones. I have found that senior managers and executives, due to their years of experience and the fact that they have been promoted through the various passages of leadership using their existing behaviors, often represent the most challenging group.

The first step is to define what is meant by a disciplined culture. As Carl outlined, my executive committee charter is included in chapter 17. Since disciplined culture has to be modelled, it has to start with me and the executive team. Is it possible to have a disciplined culture in a company with a dysfunctional, undisciplined executive team? We all know the answer to that question. The process of defining the culture starts with the vision. The culture has to support the achievement of the vision. Is Boeing more likely to value a culture of process discipline? Is Apple more likely to value a culture of innovation? At Garland, I engaged the executive team by creating a draft charter and going over every single word with the team. While this took some time and some exhausting meeting facilitation, we eventually agreed on the charter and most importantly, committed to it as a team.

Next came the hard part, which was the implementation. While we had all committed ourselves to the words on the charter, the behavior modification came quickly for some and more slowly for others. For 25% of the executive team, the change did not come at all and they had to be replaced. While they understood the importance and had verbally committed to it, they were simply too entrenched in their current behaviors to make a change. I experienced many frustrating days but during these times, I kept asking myself, "how can I change my behavior to change their behavior"? I continued to consciously focus on leading by example, holding myself and the team accountable to our disciplined culture standard. I had to use a balance of recognition by catching people doing things right and publicly acknowledging it and intervening quickly in circumstances where our standard was compromised.

Doing it was more important than saying it. Most people have been told to be honest before but in many instances, there are consequences for speaking openly. This is an important point. The foundation of a good team is trust and this can only be built through consistent behaviors. My goal was to try to lead by example by being candid, admitting where I had messed up and letting people be candid with each other without placing blame during or after the meeting. This is the most critical part. To build trust, we needed to bring our team together more often, in business and social settings. It's only through interaction that we can build trust and it has to be frequent and consistent.

While this was proving to be exhausting work for me, I developed an expectation of personal and mutual accountability amongst the team members. We agreed, as a team, not only to performing to the standard but of holding each other accountable. For this to be effective, we first had to create a climate of openness and candor where team members felt comfortable challenging, without disrespecting each other, and praising each other publicly more often. To kick start this I began to model that behavior and it caught on with the others. As this improved, the burden of transformation was now shared amongst the team members and a disciplined culture emerged.

In describing a disciplined culture we all know that small things matter. Some items might be more important than others. For example, not being on time for meetings is a good example. It is not uncommon for leaders to turn up a few minutes late almost as though a leader was entitled to this because we all know how busy he is.

As the executive team modelled the desired behaviors, this then cascaded down to all levels of the company. Formal rewards and recognition systems were implemented to promote the disciplined culture. On an annual basis, President's Awards were structured to promote the culture. Winners were selected and recognized amongst their peers. Many were promoted into new assignments.

As well as building trust, we reviewed the executive charter and set the expectation for a disciplined culture. It was up to each member to get aligned with the expectation. Broadly speaking,

I refer to the following chart in assessing and dealing with my executive team:

Category	Capable	Committed	Action
A	Capable	Committed	Develop Further
B	Capable	Not Committed	Inspire and Motivate
C	Not Capable	Committed	Coach and Reposition
D	Not Capable	Not Committed	Relocate

In developing a disciplined culture, this chart is very helpful in setting priorities and most of the leadership team will subconsciously know this chart. From a disciplined culture standpoint, because the organization is aware of this chart subconsciously, most of them would be looking at the leader to act on the people who are not performing. If the leader does not take any action, then the consequences for the organization will be dire. The culture will deteriorate and more often than not, the organization will gradually lose its best employees.

Based on the above chart, I would put the various team members in four buckets:

- Those who were capable and committed. They immediately became enablers and helped to move our company forward. My approach here was to encourage and recognize their efforts and give them more of a profile in the company.

- Then there were others who were capable but not committed. Here I worked to "enroll" them by connecting them to the broader vision and to the team goal. Over time and through business and social interaction with the team, some folded into the team. Others who found it more difficult to fully commit to a team approach left the company or had to be replaced.

- Our third grouping was not capable but committed. Here I took a personal interest in coaching and development. I relied heavily on self-assessment tools to ensure that there was a realistic realization of capability. This served as a starting point for their improvement. While some had the desire and willingness to make the changes, others accepted reassignments within the company where their capability matched the requirements of their new position.

- There is a fourth grouping which is not capable and not committed. No team members fit into this category and I would encourage everyone to take action on those who fit these criteria in your company.

As you can see, once the disciplined culture is defined, the work begins. Getting everyone aligned culturally and behaviorally is hard work. It takes time, tact, and tenacity. It's not easy stuff but your team cannot succeed without it.

In the boardrooms, offices, and hallways of Garland, you will often hear me say that when it comes to culture, our job is "to model, to promote, to nurture, and to defend". It's especially difficult to succeed when your organization is going through change, people are coming out of your company and new people are joining. For us, the team charter acts as our North Star. When you are lost in the wilderness, you pull out your compass and find the north. For us, as an executive team at Garland, it's our charter that gets us back on track and helps us find our way.

Summary of Chapter

- You may find that senior managers and executives, due to their years of experience and the fact that they have been promoted through the various passages of leadership using their existing behaviors, often represent the most challenging group to adjust to a disciplined culture.

- Ii is not possible to have a disciplined culture in a company with a dysfunctional, undisciplined executive team.

- The foundation of a good team is trust and this can only be built through consistent behaviors.

- The leader must develop an expectation of personal and mutual accountability amongst the team members.

- Formal rewards and recognition systems must be implemented to promote the disciplined culture.

- All leaders must model, promote, nurture, and defend the values and team charter.

Key Message

The leader needs the discipline to develop a disciplined culture. Once the leader's discipline is compromised, the erosion of the culture begins.

Chapter Twenty

The Fifth and Last Leadership Star
(s t a r S)
Seek and Seed Leaders at All Levels

To seek and seed leaders at all levels of an organization requires that the organization have an embedded philosophy that enthusiastically promotes the statement that "the purpose of leaders is to create more leaders." This is a simple statement, yet it is most complex to understand and implement. A great leader surrounds herself with great leaders, and a mediocre leader invariably surrounds himself with people who are less capable than he is. There are several reasons why this happens.

Firstly, there is a confidence issue. A confident leader does not hesitate to hire people who will challenge the leader. A less confident leader will tend to hire people who will be more subservient.

Secondly, a strong leader intrinsically knows that the only way she will become better is for her to surround herself with people who are strong enough to challenge her to stretch herself and seek to improve. A strong leader is normally very competitive. Just try to visualize a professional tennis player like Roger Federer choosing to practice his game with an average tennis player. This would not happen because a professional player will only ruin his game if he has to play with an average player. Similarly a great leader seeks to play with a great leader so that both of them can challenge and improve each other. This rule also clearly applies to leaders as they seek and seed their organizations with leaders at all levels.

But how many leaders truly understand this concept? How many leaders understand that the quality of their people as leaders will decide how great a leader they will be? Not too many. When they seek to recruit a person for a position, do they seek leaders who seek to create more leaders?

Why is this an issue at all? Maybe it has to do with the fact that leaders are not clearly aware that leadership means to be able to inspire others to perform better than their own expectations and not to concentrate on out performing their own people. Maybe it has to do with the fact that leadership entails empowering other leaders to outperform their own expectations, and thus ignite the leader in themselves.

Maybe it has to do with the fact that the "carrot and stick" philosophy has limited motivational effect. To really bring out the leader in people requires that a leader understand what truly motivates a person to perform at their optimum capability. Have you ever asked a keen golfer what motivates him to wake up early on a weekend to go play golf when he could be relaxing in bed on his day off? It has to do with the fact that he experiences a burst of confidence and a stronger belief in himself when he is performing at his best. This boosts his motivation to extend himself in this direction. He is responding to an inborn desire to achieve and excel. When he executes a drive on the golf course that he considers excellent, he is more than rewarded for that effort to wake up early on his day off.

People do have an inherent desire to achieve and excel. Good leaders know this intrinsically. They seek ways to make people achieve and excel and this is the essence of leadership. The good leader realizes this and creates situations for the people who work with him to excel and experience the excitement of flying high. For once the leader achieves such a situation, he knows he has created a leader, because the individual will inspire others to fly too and this is the beginning of an environment where leaders are created.

The word leader is misleading. When someone is in a position of responsibility, where she is tasked with achieving a goal through people, does she have to personally lead people or does she have to empower people to lead? We have often heard of the genius with a thousand helpers. Is such a person leading people or is that person getting others to be his ears, eyes, and hands so that he can cover a larger area by doing things himself? What of his helpers? Do they have any opportunities to use their leadership skills or are they just puppets for the use of the leaders?

When one is told that she or he is a leader, one feels compelled to be the first one out of the box to do things; to take responsibility and make things happen. There is nothing wrong with this attitude. It only goes awry when the leader thinks that he has to personally do the job rather than the fact that he has to inspire and coordinate the efforts of others. When he tries to do it all himself, he loses it. This is counterproductive. One person, no matter how good and how committed, can only achieve so much. The purpose of having an organization achieve a goal is to use all the firepower of each and every person in an organization. Therefore, the purpose of assembling an organization to achieve a goal is to optimize the capabilities and commitments of every individual in that organization. The more people have the opportunity to excel in their performance, the better the performance of the group.

The word leader does not fully convey this connotation. It screams at the individual to do things himself and not to empower a group of people to use their collective initiative and brainpower to make things happen. Can you picture one person trying her best to increase productivity and performance by working harder and for longer hours till the person drops dead with either a heart attack or a stroke or both? Better still, what is the fire power of a single great achiever compared to a group of committed and capable people working together to achieve the same goal?

The word leader tells the individual to lead and not to get others to lead. If you understand that you have to lead, the emphasis is on your performance and not the performance of those in your organization. Therefore, the word makes a person look inward and ignore the total firepower of an organization.

I have watched and interfaced with thousands of leaders in my time and the majority of them are driving themselves into the ground working long hours instead of delegating critical por- tions of their jobs so that they can do what they are supposed to do as leaders- – select and empower other leaders! These leaders often bemoan the fact that they have people under them who do not perform at their expected level. Therefore they have to fill in for them. This makes them justify the fact that they have to work so hard. Is this really a performance problem or is it a combination of poor recruitment programmes and the leader's lack of understanding of his role?

The first step in this process is to look critically at your recruit- ing process. What emphasis is placed on finding people who understand that their role is to empower others to lead? If you select people who believe their role is to achieve the best they can at any cost, then you have started the process of filling an organization full of self-centred achievers who will only create an atmosphere of unhealthy competition.

More importantly, you will fill your organization with individual performers who perform at the cost of others and in turn destroy their desire to achieve and excel. Are you then surprised when the combined efforts of your team lack cohesion and impact?

It is my experience that top leaders are also of necessity top recruiters. They are born talent scouts who when they discover a top talent, they become top salesmen for their organizations and spare no effort to convince the top talent to join their organization. Thereafter they mentor and help mould that top talent into a leader who seeks to create more leaders in the same organization.

I have seen leaders who stand by and watch while the human resource department takes months to recruit a suitable candidate for a critical position in their organization, as they throw up their hands in frustration and point to the inefficiencies of the human resource department. They don't get it that while it has something to do with the HR department's inefficiencies, it is their problem ultimately and they need to put on their organization's recruitment and salesmen hats. They need to aggressively track down the top talents in the field and pursue them relentlessly to join their organizations.

Do we always need to seek leaders in every position? My submission is that every person who is recruited is required to empower leaders whether he or she is just a single performer or a manager with a group of people who report into that person's position. This is the ideal situation. Why do I say this? Even if no one is reporting to you, you can only accelerate your performance by motivating others to do their best for the organization. This means that every person that you interface with can either make you or break you by the way they react to your requests for assistance. You, therefore, face a simple choice: every person that you recruit should of necessity believe in the philosophy that empowering others to lead is a critical requirement for their candidacy for any position. This characteristic then becomes a critical one for any recruitment for a position within an organization.

How do we emphasize the need for a leader to understand the role? By several different approaches, but mostly by promoting the motto, "the purpose of leadership is to create more leaders." This philosophy starts with the behaviour of the leader. Your behaviour as a leader will be the role model for the organization. If you as leader behave in sync with the concept that the purpose of leadership is to create more leaders, that behaviour alone will trickle down very effectively in the organization. How does this happen?

Every system and process that the organization adopts must promote this concept from recruiting to training to rewards to promotions to the behaviour of any person who is given accountability for the effective performance of the organization. This must be seriously enforced or else the philosophy will not take root.

Every leader must accept this philosophically. This is not easy to achieve in an organization. The biggest obstacle to do this lies in the fact that most leaders are slow to delegate because they are paranoid about the consequences. Tied to the concept of helping people to lead is the fact that people need a certain amount of autonomy and independence to do their own thing and gain self-confidence. Giving people the opportunity to act autonomously has tremendous rewards for an organization. Daniel Pink in his book *Drive* cites a case where researchers at Cornell University studied 320 small businesses, half of which granted workers autonomy, the other half relying on top-down direction. The businesses that offered autonomy grew at four times the rate of the control-oriented firms and had one third less turn-over.

Jacques worked hard to incorporate this philosophy in his organization. He will tell us some of the results and successes that he has had in this regard in the following chapter.

Summary of the Chapter

- Great leaders surround themselves with great people by the way they recruit them, develop them, and mentor them.

- Great leaders understand that the quality of their people will decide how effective they will be as leaders themselves.

- Leaders should understand that the key to being a good leader is to empower other people to lead rather than to jump into the lead and have others follow.

- To seek and seed leaders, organizations have to be extremely careful in their recruiting and selection practices. This is where companies can gain tremendous advantage by selecting and developing potential leaders.

- Good leaders are excellent talent scouts. They cannot and

do not depend only on the HR department to bring in good talent.

- Every individual in an organization should know and want to empower others, whether they are in leadership roles or not. Every individual who performs a job in an organization has the power to assist another and move the ball forward or block that individual and delay or even paralyse forward movement.

Key Message

You cannot be promoted if you cannot be replaced. Leaders need to constantly have their succession plans up-to-date by seeking and seeding their organizations with good leaders.

Chapter Twenty One

Leaders at All Levels of the Organization

I believe that a company cannot outgrow the capabilities of its people. In addition, the people cannot outgrow the capabilities of its leaders. For a company to win, it must have an abundance of great leaders, who in turn create more leaders.

It starts with the recruiting and selection process. It's critical that this be well executed as this is the talent that will make your company successful and become the future leaders in the company. So let's take a look at the key steps that we took at Garland:

1. Alignment with the company values. For our company the three core values were honesty, integrity, and respect. Being honest and forthright, doing what you said you would do, and treating others as you would like to be treated. While a company can succeed with many different personalities who do not always share a similar point of view, it cannot thrive unless its people share the same values. We have all heard the saying, "you get hired for what you know and fired for who you are". It's critical to ensure that values are aligned.

2. Behavioral attributes of the job. These need to be understood and listed as part of the selection criteria. For example, if we are hiring an executive assistant, we would list behaviors such as organized, punctual, efficient, and courteous, while for a customer service representative, we would include warm, friendly, positive, empathic, and accurate. Most hiring managers tend to focus solely on the technical requirements of the job and either under value or are not sufficiently trained to uncover the behaviors of the candidate. At Garland we also included leadership dimensions including "teachability" in our criteria. This is an important element of creating the leadership pipeline.

3. Technical requirements. Here we use the job description to understand the work that needs to be done and the technical capability to complete it. For example, an engineer needs to have different technical skills than an accountant. The technical skills need to be understood, listed, and validated during the selection process.

4. Team selection using behavioral interviewing. In interviewing and employee selection, consensus is king. We started by building a selection team which was made up of our strong performers who represent the best fit with your company values. Next we assigned a role to each of the team members. Some are assigned to assessing the candidates' values, others are assigned to behaviors while some are responsible for the technical. Each must work closely with the hiring manager to prepare checklists and these must be shared with the selection team ahead of the interviews. To become capable interviewers, we trained our management team on behavioral interviewing and made sure that they practiced frequently by participating on the

selection teams. The golden rule for behavioral interviewing is that past and present behavior is the best indicator of future behavior. In other words, what you see is what you get. If a candidate is acting a certain way in an interview, then you should assume that this is how they will act after you hire them. Ideally the interview process should include 2-3 interviews in different settings with different members of the selection team. Team interviewing (versus one on one) is better as team members are not always focused on asking questions and have time to observe the behavior of the candidate. After each interview is completed, the hiring manager should set up a debriefing with the selection team. In this meeting the team shares their assessment of the candidate against the job criteria. Once all the candidates have been interviewed, the team selects the person who best fits the job. I can remember many times at Garland where we were under pressure to fill an open position and almost settled for inferior candidates. This is a mistake that should be avoided and requires hiring discipline.

Once we had the talent on board, it was up to leaders to nurture and develop it. We instituted an annual talent review process to take inventory of, assess readiness, and determine development plans. We used a simple matrix in which we plotted the names of people. We have nine boxes in total, the first three marked "low performance/low potential", "low performance/medium potential", and "low performance/ high potential". The next three boxes were marked "medium performance/low potential," "medium performance/ medium potential", and "medium performance/high potential". The top three were "high performance/low potential", "high performance/medium potential", and "high performance/high potential". Each functional leader had to prepare their matrix and present it to the other members of the executive team. During this review process, the executive team gained consensus and awareness of the talent pool within our business. From there each functional leader had to develop a talent plan for their respective team members with "who/ what/by when" details. I reviewed progress with the functional leaders on a regular basis to ensure execution against actions on poor performers but most importantly, on talented people who would become our next wave of leaders.

Aside from education and training, we used team leadership and special assignments to stretch our people. The top ten high potential people were invited to join our president's council where they joined the executive committee once a quarter for an off-site meeting. They also participated in our annual strategy planning meeting and process. During this process, the president's council members experienced the challenges that the executive team faced and were able to contribute to the direction of the company. Each president's council member had an open invitation to meet with me for monthly coaching sessions. All they had to do was come forward and be prepared to work at developing themselves. I found this to be very rewarding work and enjoyed this immensely.

We also created a cross-functional, self–directed work team called change leaders. This team was comprised of high potential people and the team drove change in our business. This ranged from communicating our vision, celebrating our success or building pride in our company. Each year the team was tasked with a certain challenge and they met monthly to develop tactics and implement actions. The team had full autonomy to select and develop their plan.

Both the president's council and the change leaders teams exposed our talent to new initiatives, engaged them in building our company and developed new skills.

Each year and as part of our operating plan, we would identify our top five goals. These would be aligned to our long term strategy and short term goals. Various members of my executive team would take on the executive sponsorship role and would draw on our inventory of talent to fill the team roster. These were typically strategic projects (for example, Implement Lean/Six Sigma) that stretched our people.

To recognize our talent, we created the annual President's Awards of Excellence where we selected and recognized annual award winners. We held a gala dinner where we celebrated our award recipients. Our award recipients were recognized in company newsletters and by senior corporate management. These awards played a big part in encouraging our leaders to develop further.

Finally, the most important step was promoting from within. The culmination of all our development activities was to promote our talent into a new, progressive assignment. This validated our process and encouraged others to follow the same path.

Our job as leaders is to make new leaders. My job as the president was to be the chief talent officer. I knew that if we succeeded at the task of staffing the organization with the right talent and we had the desire, the capability, and the processes to make new leaders, our company would see fantastic success… and that's exactly what happened.

Summary of the Chapter

- A company cannot outgrow the capabilities of its people. In addition, the people cannot outgrow the capabilities of its leaders.

- Typically you get hired for what you know and fired for who you are.

- Most hiring managers tend to focus solely on the technical requirements of the job and either under value or are not sufficiently trained to uncover the behaviors of the candidate.

- In interviewing and employee selection, consensus is king.

- The golden rule for behavioral interviewing is that past and present behavior is the best indicator of future behavior. In other words, what you see is what you get.

- Institute an annual talent review process to take inventory of, assess readiness and determine development plans.

- Aside from education and training, use team leadership and special assignments to stretch your people.

- Create a cross-functional, self – directed work team, ie change leaders.

- Appoint various members of your team to take on the executive sponsorship role for key projects and stretch assignments

- Recognize your talent with the annual President's Awards of Excellence

- The most important step: whenever possible, promote from within.

Key Message

The most important role of the leader is to make new leaders.

Chapter Twenty Two

The Five Star Power Process Summarized

The Five Star Power process is so named that each step of the five steps represents a star.

The idea is that once a leader achieves all five steps, that leader is ready to take the company from good to great or be in a position to help build the company as a Five Star Power organization. In fact, leadership of an organization in these difficult economic times is the last bastion for organizations to achieve global excellence. For empowered leaders are the source of innovation and high octane performance. That is what is needed for organizations to break through to the top in these challenging times.

The first star of the Five Star Power process is the most complex and demanding star to achieve because it deals with the leader's biggest blind spot – the leader's behaviour in an organization is the model for the corporate values and culture of the organization, and not what the individual preaches. Eloquence and spouting great values might get the people's attention but not their hearts. Therefore, the first star deals with how the leader faces reality and adjusts their behaviour to set the culture that is required for the organization to reach its goals. The leader has to become the change that the leader seeks. As we all know change is easier to talk about and even simple when we tell others to adopt it, but not that easy to step up to the plate and set the example before asking others to do the same thing.

Therefore, the Five Star Power process, like most processes should, starts with the leader. If the leader employs a consultant to teach a new way of doing business to the rest of the organization and then reinforces the lessons taught by making a few inspiring speeches to the organization telling them the benefits for adopting the change, and does not subsequently adopt the change in his/her behaviour, we have a problem. Accordingly, the new process is adopted for a short period and then gradually fades into the background as everyone in the organization sees that the leader is not walking the talk. The only way to permanently embed a process in the organization is for the leader to lead the way and make the change a new way of life for the leader personally. Once this happens, everyone in the organization gets the message that the change is here to stay.

So how do we do this in the Five Star Power process? The leader is given a personal questionnaire to articulate how the leader perceives the personal strengths and weaknesses of the leader and therefore the short, medium, and long term needs of the leader. See chapter 6 (the Process-20 Questions for Leadership self Analysis, Appendix A). This questionnaire provides a profile of the leader as perceived by the leader (let's call this A).

We then provide a similar questionnaire for all the leader's direct reports, the people to whom the leader reports, the leader's customers, suppliers, and a sample of all the people in the organization. (See chapter 8, Appendix B).

This provides another profile of the same leader as seen by others. Let's call this B. Now B minus A will provide us with the gap between the two perceptions. It has been discovered through research that this gap is minimal in good leaders. Once we discover the gap, we have a developmental framework that the leader has to work with. Accordingly, the leader decides on a developmental plan. It is advisable for the leader to do this along with the help of an objective mentor or advisor. In Jacques' case I was the advisor.

The leader begins to implement the plan. It is normal for the leader to start out with a priority list and sequentially work through the list. Quite often the first item on the agenda for development is the "About Me" exercise. Through this exercise the leader is able to communicate informally with the executive team and create a platform whereby each individual is able to give and get honest feedback. Through this process the senior team is able to understand each other's strengths and weaknesses in order to be mutually supportive. The process is cascaded down to the lowest level in the organization.

One of the key side effects of this process is that the "About Me" exercise is an insidious way in which the culture of the organization changes for the better and the performance of the organization advances considerably. Also, people become more comfortable with the concept of honest and supportive feedback. This is the start of the formation of a mutually supporting team.

At this point the team needs to coalesce around a common goal. The next challenge for the leader is to help the team articulate a clear cut common vision and this is the second star, or the T, and the start of the sentence "Target the common vision and engender commitment." (See chapters 14 and 15). The leader has to enunciate the common vision – a vision that is shared by all the people in the organization. The process by which this is achieved is that every person in the organization is given a chance to express what they think the vision statement should be. Through a process of elimination and several discussions at each level of the organization, the concept is refined and finally there is a vision statement that resonates with every person in the organization and is simple and clear enough for every person to be able to relate to on a day-to-day basis.

The vision statement becomes the core of every activity that the organization undertakes. Especially when the business plan is being cast, it works backwards from the vision statement. When people undertake any task which leaves them in doubt as to what course to follow, they refer to the vision statement and get back on track. They refer to the vision statement when dealing with customers, suppliers, stakeholders and use the vision statement to define the organization's reason for being. Most importantly, every person should be able to repeat the vision statement since it should be simple enough and so inspiring that they would be excited and proud to repeat it.

The leader now moves on to the third star, or A, which is the first letter in the sentence "Assemble mutually supporting teams." (See chapters 16 and 17). This is dependent on the leader again. The leader has to model the behaviour that he seeks to embed in a team. Of course, the first step is to define the behaviour and get acceptance at all levels of the organization for this behaviour which is treated as a charter that can be constantly referred to on a day-to-day basis.

Thereafter, the leader walks the talk first and the executive team sets the example for the rest of the organization. The core of this behaviour is that the team is mutually supportive and mutually responsible for the effectiveness of the organization.

This star is where the rubber hits the road because now things become very tangible for the rest of the organization. The team has to take responsibility for implementing the business plan as a team with a strong focus on the vision. The leader has to monitor the activity very closely without hindering the use of innovation. The leader's true test is to let the team evolve spontaneously and only intervene when the team is veering away from the agreed charter and/ or forgetting their commitments to their agreed upon vision.

This brings us to the next star, or R, standing for "Reward a disciplined culture." See chapters 18 and 19. The difference between a great performing team and an average performing team is discipline. This aspect is very obvious when an organization is under pressure to deliver. The leader's challenge over here is to define a disciplined code of conduct and reward any conduct that reflects this code. The greatest challenge is for the leader to follow this code without blinking, especially under pressure. No exceptions. Period.

We now come to the last and very critical star. This is the last S of the Five Star Power process. It is also the first letter in the sentence, "Seek and Seed innovative leaders at all levels of the organization." Please see chapters 20 and 21. This star is critical because everything that happens in an organization is initiated by a leader at some level. If there is a paucity of leadership in an organization, the lack of performance will soon make the organization redundant. Every leader's motto should be, "the purpose of leaders is to create more leaders" and along with this motto, the leader should be a true believer in the concept that no organization can rise above the capabilities of its leaders. Armed with these two precepts, any leader will rethink all processes from leadership recruiting to leadership development, leadership succession, rewards and promotions, and so on.

We now have a an easy acronym to guide us through the process along with attached simple sentences to remind us what each letter stands for. The acronym is STARS and each letter stands for:

- Start operating in the real world personally.

- Target the common vision and engender commitment.

- Assemble mutually supporting teams.

- Reward a disciplined culture.

- Seek and Seed innovative leaders at all levels of an organization.

This is a simple acronym for leaders to remember and follow through in any organization. If a leader follows this simple process, which challenges the very roots of the leader's beliefs and expands the leader's personal horizons as well as the horizons of those who work with the leader, the results should be as spectacular as recorded in this book; and if not as spectacular, it will definitely raise the bar of performance and the organization's profile significantly. More importantly, you as a leader will have the satisfaction of firing on all cylinders as a person.

Chapter Twenty Three

Reaching Beyond the FIVE STAR POWER Process

Y ou have nearly made it to the end of the book but you are at the beginning of implementation. As we have explained, it is a sequential process that takes a fair amount of time and patient persistence. As you implement the process, the rewards become immediately tangible to everyone: you, the people in the organization, your customers, suppliers, and all stakeholders. This should serve as a strong motivator as it builds enthusiasm and encouragement for all during the process. This enthusiasm should not wane as all five stars are finally completed. Normally people tend to think that the process will take care of itself and that the organization will continue to move forward on the strength of the process. While this is true to an extent, the fact is that the process has to be implemented by people and people need to move forward using the process as a foundation.

What this means is that the leaders in the organization have to step up to the plate in a big way once execution starts. While responsibilities are allocated and champions and sponsors are appointed, each leader now has to work harder than ever to move the people forward. This is because the appointed leaders normally have to deal with a grass roots change in behaviour.

They now have to use different tools and processes to help the teams understand, accept, and apply the new rules of engagement. This requires a deeper understanding of the role of a leader. Actually there are three critical roles of a leader during a period of rapid change:

- The orchestrator.

- The coach.

- The cheerleader.

The Orchestrator

The leader creates light, not heat. What does this phrase mean? It means that the leader is a beacon of light for the team. The leader is a like a minesweeper clearing the way for an advancing army. The army continues to advance because the minesweeper has made it easier for the army to advance, but nothing more. In other words, the leader orchestrates situations so that the team can get the task done, leaving the team to use their initiative as they overcome obstacles along the way. I have seen leaders who stand in judgement of their team as the pressure increases, instead of coaxing and guiding the team through the rapids. I have heard someone say of a leader that he would throw an untethered rope to a drowning person. I do not think any leader does that knowingly. But the leader may as well be doing that by criticizing people and threatening them with dire consequences if they fail, and that is not what an orchestrator does. An orchestrator is always thinking ahead for the team and therefore avoids the drowning incident, even helping the team to avoid the rapids by the simple act of asking the team the right question. The orchestrator has the team's back. The orchestrator creates trust and confidence in the team. The orchestrator takes time to connect the dots for people who interpret the new rules of engagement differently than what was intended, and further demonstrates the concept by becoming the change that is sought by the organization, and therefore models the behaviour.

The orchestrator knows that it is more important to ask the right question rather than to give the right answer. The team needs to grow and develop its skills at solving problems by the leader asking the team the right probing questions. Most leaders fall into the trap of giving the team the answer when the team comes up against an obstacle. All this does is make the team more and more dependent on the leader, thereby losing what initiative and creative talents they possess. If we accept that the key role of a leader is to create more leaders then the orchestrator concentrates on building leaders in the team, even as the team is working to solve a problem.

To orchestrate is to eschew micromanaging. The orchestrator needs time to look at the task in the light of the possible pitfalls that the team will encounter as they undertake the task. Having identified these pitfalls, the leader orchestrates it so that the team is forewarned and prepared to cope with the obstacles as they occur.

Therefore, to orchestrate effectively one has to be able to clearly see patterns as circumstances develop. What do I mean by seeing patterns? As a situation unfolds while a team is working on a task, the orchestrator sees a pattern developing that points to a certain conclusion that either needs to be exploited or avoided, then alerts the team to this by asking the right questions of the team. For instance, I have been in sales meetings where a sales team will claim that things are on track by being over optimistic of the sales status. If the leader does not alert the team to this misconception by asking meaningful questions as early as possible, the sales situation will continue down a never ending slippery slope to disaster. The orchestrator who does this is being a minesweeper for the team.

Another role that the orchestrator plays is of being the person who is the interpreter for the team upwards to the next level of leadership and also the interpreter for the higher level leaders to the team. This makes for the least amount of misunderstanding and confusion in communication, interpretation and subsequent implementation.

The last if not least role that the orchestrator plays is one of being the official tracker and conscience of the team. The team is disciplined to deliver what they promise and the orchestrator sets a personal example by delivering against commitments.

The Coach

The coach is not unlike what we traditionally understand a coach does in sports. The main theme that the coach uses to coach the team is to remember that the coach does not play in the big game, the team does. What this means is that the coach must so prepare the team that it can function effectively and independently when the pressure is on them.

The first and most important role for a coach is to assess the team's capability to achieve the organization's stated vision. The coach decides whether the team has the competence to deliver against the company's vision. Once this is clear then the coach reviews if each role is correctly occupied by the right person. Finally, the coach should ascertain that every person on the team is clearly committed to achieving the stated vision. They're not too different from a coach as we know it in the sports world.

The coach is the talent scout for the team. This is a very important skill that all good leaders should have. The leader should first and foremost be a skilled recruiter who is constantly on the lookout for top talent to lure into one of the seats on the team bus. The bus seats of the team should be always well occupied with backups in readiness to fill any vacated seat. This is just good succession planning.

The next key function that the coach has is to keep the team well-tuned and constantly at peak training. This is often overlooked in an organization where training is treated more like a luxury rather than a necessity. In this day things change at the blink of an eye. A team that is not abreast with the latest will not be competitive and lose out.

The next function is that the team needs to be well disciplined and clearly focused on an objective. The coach has to simplify any targeted activity by connecting the dots from a vision statement or goal to the daily activity of the team. At the same time, the coach must be able to generate an atmosphere of trust, especially in an informal setting.

The coach is a friend and a confidante of the team. Each member of the team is individually coached and mentored to perform above and beyond the individual's expectations. The coach essentially makes it happen. The next key role of the leader expands on this concept.

The Cheerleader

The cheerleader is the inveterate motivator. Every team has its ups and downs and the cheerleader has to be sensitive to the moods of the team. While the coach pushes for top results, the cheerleader cajoles and coaxes them over the bumps. The cheerleader is constantly on the lookout for the efforts of team members that can be recognized and praised. Good team members are often very sensitive and usually have big egos. The cheerleader knows when to feed those egos and address sensitive issues in a timely fashion.

The cheerleader has to have a sense of humour and know how to lighten up the team's spirits and raise their morale. A team that is down cannot perform at their optimum. The team needs to lighten up and focus. This is where the cheerleader is most needed.

Essentially, the cheerleader is the humane side of the leader. The cheerleader is a master in informal settings where each team member's personal needs are considered by the leader and given a sympathetic and supportive ear. Here is where the cheerleader helps the team see the cup as half full and not half empty. It is a proven fact that when an individual believes in himself/herself and sees the positive side of any situation, there is a better chance for that individual to achieve greater results.

These three roles are not easy to attain and most leaders may have two roles mastered but only have a sprinkling of the third. This is fine as long as the leader is aware of this missing link, and is working on this deficiency. This is way better than having just one of the three roles mastered and a sprinkling of the other two.

The Five Star Power process is very demanding of leaders but is also very powerful in raising the performance and quality of leaders and their organizations to heights that most people would not be able to achieve without it. Hundreds of leaders and dozens of organizations can witness to this fact.

The difference between successfully implementing the Five Star Power process and not is the effectiveness with which the leaders of the organization perform the above three roles as they become the change they seek.

As Sir Winston Churchill said after the defeat of Rommel in the Egyptian desert, "This is not the end. This is not the beginning of the end. It is perhaps the end of the beginning." The book you have just read is the end of the beginning. You are now ready to practice what we preached and delivered in the FIVE STAR POWER process. It is the start of a journey that will take you to heights that neither you nor your organization nor the stakeholders of your organization ever visualized.

Summary of the Chapter

- This is the beginning of the implementation of the Five Star Power process, where the rubber really hits the road.

- Hence the leaders of the organization need to really step up to the plate as leaders. They have to effectively perform three critical roles:

- The orchestrator – clears the way for the team to achieve its goals.

- The coach – functions exactly as a coach of a sports team.

- The cheerleader – the chief motivator for the team.

- Most effective leaders have mastered these three roles. It may be possible to function with at least two of these roles while developing the third role. If a leader can function only in one of these roles, the Five Star Power process will not be effectively sustained.

Key Message

To maintain a high performing team, the leader needs to be a high performing leader.

Chapter Twenty Four

Sustaining Momentum After The Five Star Power Process

One of the trappings of success is thinking that you have reached the pinnacle of achievement and that you can relax. While we certainly celebrated and enjoyed the great results that the Five Star Power process delivered, I felt that a healthy paranoia needed to continue to exist in our company. If not, we could fall back to our old ways. While we had accomplished much, I also felt that our company and our team had great long term potential. To realize this we needed to sustain and build on our accomplishments. While we had been working to become a five star company for years, I felt that it was almost like a rubber band. One can stretch it, but as soon as you let go, it snaps back to its original shape and size. I did not want that to happen at Garland. Keeping the Five Star Power process front and center and executing against each element is the key to sustaining the gains and taking your company to the next level. I repeated the steps in the Five Star Power process over and over again and utilized the tools and, based on my experiences, added a few others along the way:

- Continuing to operate in the real world. Let's face it, glo-balization and technology are driving a dizzying pace of change so it's sometimes hard to figure out what the real world is. If you do, it's likely to change tomorrow. I found myself having to do extensive reading to keep up. I read two newspapers every morning, one book, and approximately. twenty magazines every month. That's on top of my 100+ daily e-mails. I believe that understanding what is happening in the outside world is a key part of my job as well as that of my executive team.

- One tool that I rely on heavily is agony. I believe that on the other side of agony, is reality. When I coach or mentor people, I often tell them to "follow their agony". Usually the thing that is creating the most agony for that leader is the thing that they should face first. It's causing the blockage in their performance. It could be a new competitor, an employee, or a customer issue. If you are agonizing about it, it probably means that you have not fully faced your reality. When I focus on my agony and successfully overcome it, it usually leads to a significant breakthrough. Try it.

- Of course, keep asking for feedback from your team and schedule 360 feedback sessions every 3-5 years.

- Promoting the common vision and engendering commitment to it. Sometimes I wondered if I was overdoing it, repeating our vision over and over again. Just when I thought I could back off a bit, I talked to someone in our company who didn't have a clue what we are trying to do. It was a new employee or someone who missed out on key communication sessions. So I stepped up my efforts. In every newsletter, in every town hall meeting, there's our vision statement. I started and ended each of my presentations with the vision statement. Every year we got our team involved in reviewing the vision and updating the strategy. We got that same team together once a quarter to discuss progress and make adjustments. Once our team was clear on the direction, I had to ensure that we were taking action against it. This is where we developed our top five goals for each year, which moved us closer to the achievement of our vision. I continually assigned executive sponsorship for each of the goals to one specific member of the executive team. Most of the time I selected a direct report that would grow or develop most from this assignment.

- When it comes to your vision, how to do you know if your people are getting it? When you are interacting with people on your team, ask them if they can recite your vision. Then ask them what it means and if they are inspired by it. Thirdly, ask them if they understand how their personal contribution will help make it a reality. If each employee in your company can get through the three questions without hesitation, you have achieved something that most companies will never do. Pat yourself on the back but keep working at it!

- Building mutually supportive teams. Talk about hard work. I found myself constantly monitoring individual and team behaviors to see how effective we were. On any given day, someone or one of our teams was exhibiting unusual behavior and I had to intervene to get to the root cause. With so many team activities going on in the business, I inserted myself into meetings or scheduled reviews to see how the teams were doing. I set expectations for teamwork and held people accountable for it. Building the team is something that I worked on every day. It's like a professional sports team who is constantly working on their roster. Promoting and demoting. Constantly tweaking to find the ultimate position for specific players and looking for ways to maximize team performance.

- I spent a good portion of my time coaching leaders on interview preparation and then participating with them in interviews, candidate assessment, and selection. By participating in the process, our leaders learned and practiced the behavioral interviewing and I could see them using their new found skills over and over again. As a team, the more capable we got at understanding people, the more confident we were in making faster and better decisions on hiring and firing.

- Rewarding a disciplined culture. I must admit that at times I find myself wanting to take short cuts. I want things to happen quickly to get to the benefit. It rarely works that way. So the real challenge for me was to maintain my own personal discipline. As our business processes evolved, we wrote them down and shared them with others. Again, repetition is key so our team needed to understand how we did the work and then use that same process, over and over again. One of the best tools we used was the balanced scorecard. In it, we had different metrics and we tracked our progress on a monthly basis. Some of the metrics included customer satisfaction, on time delivery, profit, cash flow, warranty, gross margins, first time fix rates on our equipment repairs, employee satisfaction, credit notes, number of training sessions held, delivery lead times, profit per employee, inventory turns, collections, factory quality, number of patents, time to answer a telephone call, abandoned call rates, absenteeism, safety rates, positions filled internally, number of celebrations held, voluntary departure rates, percentage of employee performance feedback sessions completion, and productivity. At our monthly executive committee meeting and during our quarterly off-site meetings with the president's council, we reviewed each line of our scorecard and discussed the underlying performance.

- Seeding and seeking innovative leaders at all levels. For me this was the most fun and gratifying aspect of the Five Star Power process. I really enjoyed watching our team grow and individual team members develop. While my primary focus was on the development of my direct reports, I personally coached a few of our high potential people. While we had many people working with internal and external coaches on their development, I made the early mistake of not moving them quickly enough into new positions or giving them stretch project assignments. That mistake cost us as we lost some of our best talent. On more than one occasion I have heard people say, "if we invest in the development of our people, they are going to leave so why bother". While that can certainly happen, and it did at Garland in a few instances, it was because we did not take deliberate action to move our talent into new and challenging assignments. I blamed myself for this mistake and once we made the corrections in our talent management process, our retention rates improved dramatically as did our business results. A second key learning for me is that it was not solely my responsibility to develop the talent. I believe that one of the key responsibilities of a leader is to develop new leaders. It started with me setting an expectation with my direct reports which then cascaded down to the balance of the leadership team.

Next I ran into another unexpected hurdle. Many of our leaders did not know how to develop new leaders. So I found myself coaching my team on coaching their teams. The steps I used included building trust, envisioning the end state, identifying the blockages to achieving that end state, creating a personal action plan, and developing new skills by practicing them in real life situations. Think of it as a teacher who is not only teaching the students but is also teaching the teachers how to teach.

By staying true to the principles of the Five Star Power process and driving repetition, you can not only sustain the gains but lift your teams' performance to even higher levels. Don't worry about getting stuck on a plateau. By developing an inspiring vision that constantly stretches your team and combining it with the Five Star Power process, the sky is the limit!

Summary of the Chapter

- One of the trappings of success is thinking that you have reached the pinnacle of achievement and that you can relax.

- To find reality and the next breakthrough, follow your agony.

- Repeat your vision over and over until everyone gets it.

- As a team, the more capable you are at understanding people, the more confident you are in making faster and better decisions on hiring and firing.

- Develop a balanced scorecard to track your progress.

- Take deliberate action to move your talent into new and challenging assignments or risk losing them.

- The leader must teach the teachers how to teach.

Key Message

You are never done. Keep working on the Five Star Process to reach new heights.

Chapter Twenty Five

The Results – Where the Rubber Hits the Road

I have to be honest in saying that when Carl first approached me about writing the book, my initial reaction was to say no. It sounded like hard work and why would someone want to hear my story? Since Carl had not led me astray on the Five Star Power process and I trusted him, I agreed to do it. What I learned in the process is that writing the book is in itself a part of becoming a better leader. After more than twenty years of work, to pause and think back on the things that made me successful, it made me more conscious of the elements and more capable of applying my formula to improve Garland or any business for that matter. How many people have you met who have been wildly successful but when asked how they did it, they respond with, "I don't really know, luck I guess". How many people do you know who are struggling to improve their businesses or their leadership skills and don't know where to start? Being able to clearly understand, articulate, and apply a formula is unusual and a skill that is highly sought after.

In the preceding chapters, Carl and I have shared with you the theory, the practical application, and some of the hurdles you will encounter in implementing the Five Star Power process.

From my perspective, there are three key stakeholders who will benefit from the process and this book:

(a) I, as a Co-author,

I benefited immensely from the process of discovery that it took to write this book. I feel more confident and capable as a leader and more grounded as a person. To be a good leader, you have to be consistent in your behaviour all the time. This means that the process helped me to not only improve my skills as a leader, it helped me to improve my behaviour. This gives me a feeling of self-fulfillment and self-actualization. The process gave me a new, energetic perspective on life and reality. I highly recommend it.

(b) The Business

Secondly, our business benefited from the FIVE STAR POWER Process. From 2004 to 2008, Garland experienced:

- EBITA improvement of 175%.

- Cash flow improvement of 254%.

- Employee satisfaction of 85%.

- 16% reduction in absenteeism.

- 54% improvement in safety.

- Organic sales growth of 52%.

More importantly, Garland outperformed the industry by more than three times. The process left the company in an excellent healthy condition.

(c) You, the Reader

And the third and final stakeholder is you, our reader. It is our sincere hope that by sharing the Five Star Power process and its implementation, you can unleash your companies' secret weapon, its leaders, giving your organization an unprecedented shot in the arm and a taste of success and pride. Apart from that, you will give yourself the opportunity to grow immensely as a leader and as an individual.

While the Five Star Power process led the way for us, I would be remiss in not thanking the people at Garland for their hard work. Their passion for excellence is unrivalled in our industry. While it was hard work, the team rose to the challenge, adapted and persevered through some tough challenges. They supported me in my leadership development. They are truly a world class team and I am proud to be associated with each and every member of the Garland family.

Carl Phillips is a great friend and teacher. He has and continues to make his mark in the field of personal development and global organizational effectiveness. My sincere thanks to Carl for guiding me through this process and for his support along the way. Thanks to both our families who supported us as we implemented the process and wrote the book.

As I reflect on what we accomplished, it brings me back to the roots of my philosophy as I described it in chapter 3. What had shaped me as a child was being put into practice through the Five Star Power process. So while it was difficult, it felt comfortable at the same time. After searching for years to find the secret to business and personal success, the Five Star Power process transformed me and our company.

20 Steps to the FIVE STAR POWER Process:

1. "Your story" – summary of events that shaped your life.

2. Leadership self analysis questionnaire.

3. 360 feedback process.

4. Feedback plan of action.

5. Detailed personal development plan.

6. "About Me" summary write up.

7. Develop the vision statement.

8. Define and communicate company values.

9. Develop the executive team charter.

10. Capabilities and commitment matrix.

11. Add behaviors to employee selection criteria.

12. Training on behavioral interviewing.

13. Complete talent matrix.

14. Introduce president's council.

15. Appoint change champions (ie. Change leaders).

16. Executive sponsorship of top five annual goals.

17. Develop a balanced scorecard.

18. Annual review of Five Star Power process.

19. Complete your 360 feedback session every 3-5 years with your coach to help sustain your gains.

20. Celebrate and enjoy your team's success.

Be a winner and don't be lonely at the top!

About the Authors

Carl a Phillips, MA, CMC

Carl Phillips, a Certified Management Consultant, retired as Head of The Global Organization Effectiveness Practice of Watson Wyatt Worldwide. Previous to that he was Founder and CEO of The Phillips Group, a leading Management Consulting Company specializing in Organization Effectiveness. With offices in Canada and the USA, Carl serviced many Fortune 500 Companies with their leadership needs. In 1993 Watson Wyatt Worldwide acquired The Phillips Group, and appointed Carl Global Head of the Organization Effectiveness Practice.

In this role, he Co-Authored the book "Global Literacies," a book on Global leadership Culled from 75 CEOs of prestigious Global Organizations. "Winners Are Not Lonely At The Top" is his second book on Leadership Effectiveness and is rooted in a lifetime of experience helping leading companies improve their performances exponentially through the Five Star Power process.

Carl has been married to Maureen for 46 years and the couple have two children, Alison and Shane. They also have two Grandchildren, Troy and Ashley.

Carl and Maureen live in Oakville, Ontario, Canada.

Jacques Seguin

Jacques spent 27 years in various roles at Garland under four different parent companies. Jacques started his career at the entrance level of the organization and worked his way through progressive assignments with the last 12 years in general management. Jacques is currently in a general management role at Garland and applying the FIVE STAR POWER process. Jacques remains active in his industry and is a Director and Past Chair of the Canadian Hospitality Foundation to advance education for those seeking careers in the hospitality industry. He is a Fellow of the Ontario Hostelry Institute.

Jacques has personally undergone the Five Star Power process and his organization has outperformed their industry by more than three times. Jacques is passionate about Leadership Development and he has had impressive successes practicing it.Jacques has been married to Michele for 25 years and the couple have two children, Jacob and Jared.

Jacques and Michele live in Mississauga, Ontario, Canada.

Jacques Seguin on left, Carl Phillips on right

CPSIA information can be obtained
at www.ICGtesting.com
Printed in the USA
BVHW070945110319
542311BV00008B/109/P